DEATH WINS IN THE ARCTIC

DEATH WINS IN THE ARCTIC

The Lost Winter Patrol of 1910

Kerry Karram

DUNDURN
TORONTO

Editors: Jane Gibson and Jennifer McKnight
Design: Jesse Hooper
Printer: Webcom

Library and Archives Canada Cataloguing in Publication

Karram, Kerry, author
    Death wins in the arctic : the lost winter patrol of 1910 / by Kerry Karram.

Based on Francis Joseph Fitzgerald's daily journal records.
Includes bibliographical references and index.
Issued in print and electronic formats.
ISBN 978-1-4597-1753-4 (pbk.).--ISBN 978-1-4597-1754-1 (pdf).--ISBN 978-1-4597-1755-8 (epub)

    1. Fitzgerald, Francis J., 1869-1911--Travel--Northwest Territories. 2. Fitzgerald, Francis J., 1869-1911--Death and burial. 3. Royal North West Mounted Police (Canada)--Officials and employees--Travel--Northwest Territories. 4. Dogsledding--Northwest Territories--History--20th century. 5. Northwest Territories--Description and travel. 6. Northwest Territories--History--1905-1951. I. Title.

FC3216.2.K37 2013   971.9'102   C2013-905479-0
                                    C2013-905480-4

1 2 3 4 5   17 16 15 14 13

We acknowledge the support of the **Canada Council for the Arts** and the **Ontario Arts Council** for our publishing program. We also acknowledge the financial support of the **Government of Canada** through the **Canada Book Fund** and **Livres Canada Books**, and the **Government of Ontario** through the **Ontario Book Publishing Tax Credit** and the **Ontario Media Development Corporation**.

Care has been taken to trace the ownership of copyright material used in this book. The author and the publisher welcome any information enabling them to rectify any references or credits in subsequent editions.

J. Kirk Howard, President

The publisher is not responsible for websites or their content unless they are owned by the publisher.

Printed and bound in Canada.

VISIT US AT
Dundurn.com | *@dundurnpress* | *Facebook.com/dundurnpress* | *Pinterest.com/dundurnpress*

Dundurn	Gazelle Book Services Limited	Dundurn
3 Church Street, Suite 500	White Cross Mills	2250 Military Road
Toronto, Ontario, Canada	High Town, Lancaster, England	Tonawanda, NY
M5E 1M2	L41 4XS	U.S.A. 14150

To Andrew, Victoria, and Mikaela
"Love's greatest gift: remembrance"

Contents

Foreword

During the late 1800s, Canada was still in its infancy as a new country. The Canadian government had just purchased a large area of land known as Rupert's Land, as well as the Northwest Territory from the Hudson's Bay Company. This newly acquired land, however, was not without its problems.

The West was a lawless area. The first of two rebellions led by Louis Riel had just been put down in 1869. Intertribal warfare among the Native people, marked by the stealing of horses and collecting of scalps, was commonplace. The situation was exacerbated by the incursion of American whisky traders who were ruthless in their pursuit of buffalo robes from the Natives through the illegal trade of rot-gut whisky. Often a whole buffalo hide was traded for one cup of the illegal "whisky," which would contain, among other ingredients, but not limited to: tobacco juice (sometimes from a spittoon), red ink, Jamaican Ginger, spices, and just enough strychnine to make the Natives sick. Seemingly, they suspected they were getting ripped off if they did not get sick.

Prime Minister Sir John A. Macdonald had promised this new country, the newly created Dominion of Canada, that he would connect the East to the West by means of a railway. Behind the promise lay multiple obvious concerns of trying to build in such a lawless and dangerous area. Something had to be done. Macdonald had received a report that a force of one hundred to 150 mounted riflemen could both establish and maintain law and order. Inspired by the likes of the Royal Irish Constabulary, as well as the Mounted Rifle units of the United States Army, the prime minister decided to pursue the idea of a similar Canadian force.

The possibility was discussed after the purchase of Rupert's Land, but three years later there was still no progress. A single event would be the catalyst to make this idea a reality. On June 1, 1873, news from the Cypress Hills (near present day Maple Creek, Saskatchewan) that a gang of white wolf hunters had massacred a camp of Assiniboine Indians made national and international news. The Canadian government feared that without a strong presence of law and order they could find themselves involved in an expensive war with the Natives, similar to that happening in the neighbouring United States. There were also concerns over sovereignty since American whisky traders were making themselves at home on Canadian soil, corrupting the Natives with illegal booze, and flying American flags over their posts. The government needed to act, and needed to act fast.

On May 23, 1873, an act for the establishment of the North West Mounted Police passed through parliament — unopposed. Originally John A. MacDonald wanted to call the force the "North West Mounted Rifles," but out of concern that the United States might see this as a military buildup, he renamed it the "North West Mounted Police."

This legislation was the beginning of what eventually would become one of the most famous police forces in the world. Approved by an order in council on August 30, 1873, this predecessor of the Royal Canadian Mounted Police (RCMP), the North West Mounted Police (NWMP), were officially created and were to be ready to start as soon as possible. Their duty was to travel west and once there, wipe out the illegal whisky trade, suppress lawlessness, protect the workers of the new railway being built, assist new homesteaders to the area, develop peaceful relations with the Native people, and establish Canadian sovereignty. This was a tall order for what was originally going to be 150 men. It was soon realized that this number of men would be insufficient for the task ahead. The force's first permanent commissioner, George A. French, recruited an additional three troops, totalling 150 men, from eastern Canada. These recruits left Toronto in June 1874, travelling by rail through Chicago to Fargo, North Dakota. There, they disembarked and marched northward across the border to join up with the original three troops at the small boundary settlement of Fort Dufferin.

On July 8, 1874, approximately 275 officers and men, with horses and equipment, left Fort Dufferin, Manitoba, in a single caravan that stretched for miles to head farther west. They arrived in present-day southern Alberta in October of that same year, having completing the longest march ever undertaken by a British regiment — a distance of 1,959 miles. A lack of supplies and inadequate food and water were only a few of the problems they encountered. How they managed to even reach their destination is a story in itself.

However, it was that determination to finish the job that was started, despite the odds or the difficulty, that quickly earned the young force a stellar reputation that would go on to become legendary. That determination would be tested time and time again throughout the ensuing years as new challenges, stemming from the difficulty of policing such a vast area of land at times under some of the harshest conditions on the planet, arose from time to time.

In 1895, the jurisdiction of the NWMP was extended to the Yukon. Three years later, in 1898, gold was discovered in the Yukon, and fortune-seeking people headed to the North in droves, hoping to strike it rich. Although many were there to seek wealth legitimately, there were almost as many looking to get rich off of those who found fortune. Once again, the force was put to the test in its ability to keep the peace without resorting to violence in its firm yet fair approach to everything.

In 1903 a dispute arose over the Alaska boundary between the United States and British colony of Canada. The judicial council arbitrators decided in favour of the Americans. This decision caused Ottawa to become concerned about both American and foreign whalers who were very active in the northern Arctic waters. Would they become a threat to the Canadian sovereignty along the Arctic coastlines and the surrounding islands? A series of detachments and a patrol network were established so the NWMP could extend its authority and a Canadian presence all the way to the Arctic coast.

In the fall of 1903, Superintendent Charles Constantine, Sergeant Francis Fitzgerald, and four constables were ordered to proceed to Fort McPherson, located in the Northwest Territories at the mouth of the Mackenzie River, to establish the NWMP's first real presence north of the Arctic Circle. Sergeant Fitzgerald continued on to Herschel Island in the Arctic Ocean. He reported that Canada was losing tax revenue, which was not being collected from whalers. He further reported that while wintering on the island, the whalers were supplying the Eskimo (known today as Inuit) with liquor. Fitzgerald quickly made it clear to the captains of the whaling ships that this supplying of "booze" would stop and that duties were to be paid on all good brought into Canada. Fitzgerald spent the next six years at Herschel Island. During that time his only communication with the outside world was with the whalers who came to the island.

By 1904, King Edward VII bestowed the prefix title of "Royal" to the Force in recognition of their diligent service to "King and Country." The newly named Royal Northwest Mounted Police had now established a system of regular winter dog-team patrols for the North to keep an eye over this extended part of the country.

Six years later, in 1910, the newly promoted Inspector Fitzgerald was now a veteran of the North and of the force. He was excited at having been selected to be part of the contingent to be sent over to England for the coronation of King George V, scheduled for July 1911. In order to get out of the North by a date that would enable him to travel to Britain in time, it was decided that Fitzgerald would head the annual winter patrol between Dawson and Fort McPherson, except this year it would leave from Fort McPherson and travel to Dawson. Being somewhat competitive, possibly anxious for his trip to England, or perhaps overconfident, Fitzgerald most likely saw the trip as an opportunity to break the record for time of previous patrols.

This may be just one of many possible reasons that an experienced Mountie of the North decided to pack lightly by reducing the amount of food and equipment he took with him for this patrol. Whatever the reason, it was a fatal mistake he would not live to tell. Despite the unwavering determination for which the force has been become legendary, the hostile and unforgiving climate of the North showed without a doubt that determination is often not enough for one to survive in the North.

Through the carefully chosen words of author Kerry Karram, readers will feel as though they are along for the ride as part of this ill-fated patrol that will forever be known in both RCMP and Canadian history as the "The Lost Patrol." You will quickly begin to appreciate what members of the force were exposed to on a daily basis of what could easily be a script for an extreme reality show. This, in fact, was just the daily routine for these men. Kerry gives you more than just the details of this tragic event — she gives you an experience that reaches out to all your senses. Kerry is a proud Canadian and a proud parent of a Mountie. She has a real passion for Canadian history and wants to share these sometimes obscure or forgotten stories from history of ordinary people doing extraordinary things. Her passion is contagious and will leave you craving more.

I have read the official reports about this event. I have read Fitzgerald's actual diary, and the details of this are well documented. Many members of the RCMP are aware of this event, but only a very few of the general public know some of the details. Even fewer know of the hardship, bravery, and determination faced by four ordinary men doing the extraordinary. Yet this story has rarely been told outside of the RCMP archive records. Kerry breathes new life into this forgotten part of Canadian history. So sit back, bundle up, and prepare for an incredible journey.

Corporal Sean Chiddenton
Regimental #45468
Drill Instructor, Royal Canadian Mounted Police
Depot Division, Regina, Saskatchewan

Acknowledgements

After my visit to The Royal Canadian Mounted Police Heritage Centre, at Depot in Regina, Saskatchewan, on the occasion of my son's graduation, I didn't spend much time contemplating the idea of writing the story of the Lost Patrol of 1910. That part was easy; it was a story I wanted to tell. What followed was the dedicated involvement of many people to make my vision become real, and I am grateful for the constant support I was given as each page was written, each fact was checked, and each question answered. The story you are about to read could not have been written without the help of many.

It is true to say that this book would not have been written without Corporal Sean Chiddenton, Drill, Deportment and Tactical Unit at Depot, Regina. Sean was a driving force behind the project. His passion to preserve the history of the North West Mounted Police, the Royal Northwest Mounted Police, and the Royal Canadian Mounted Police spills into his training of new cadets, and that is how my son, Constable Andrew Karram, was first made aware of the Lost Patrol and in turn his suggesting that I must meet Corporal Chiddenton. Sean is the person who first shared the diary of Inspector F.J. Fitzgerald and in doing so inspired *Death Wins in the Arctic*. He was my guide during this journey.

In Corporal Chiddenton's early years with the Royal Canadian Mounted Police, he was posted "North of 60" in the Northwest Territories, where he received the Commissioners Commendation for Bravery. Having lived near the Arctic Circle for many years, Sean was able to give me insights to what life in the North is like. Time and again he found sources for me after I sent him email messages with the subject line "Help!" It is no wonder he received the Queen's Diamond Jubilee medal in 2012, as his dedication to the force he proudly represents is exemplary. Thank you, Sean, for also writing the Foreword. My gratitude for your continual enthusiasm and expertise knows no bounds.

I am also indebted and give my warmest thanks to Jane Gibson and Barry Penhale both of whom once again showed they believed in me, and who presented the idea for *Death Wins in the Arctic* to Dundurn Press. Jane, I deeply appreciate your insightful and valuable comments on my manuscript, which breathed life into the narrative and Barry, I gratefully acknowledge your confidence in my ability to tell the story, and your belief in its importance to Canadians. I could not be more fortunate in having two such experienced and extraordinary advisors working with me. Your encouragement and counsel were invaluable. Thank you.

Marti Sevier — thank you once again for your willingness to sit for hours and hours reading and rereading draft after draft and "polishing" the words I wrote. I know we "shivered" together as we imagined the frigid temperatures the Lost Patrol endured, and also "laboured" as they did, as they struggled up mountains. Sometimes I felt as though we were actually there! Thank you for everything. I could easily have been "lost" without you.

Thank you Jennifer McKnight, my copy editor. Working with you once was fantastic, but twice? How was I so lucky!

My thanks are also due to Beth Dempster, Jack Dempster's granddaughter, not only for drawing the excellent maps in this book, but also for sharing your knowledge of the region where the early Mounties made their patrols. It must have been an unsettling experience to travel along parts of the route where the Lost Patrol made their way so many decades ago. At the same time, to drive along the highway named after your grandfather must be so gratifying. It has been a privilege to work with you and to have you be a part of this story. I am certain Jack would be proud that his granddaughter continues to honour his memory and lead expeditions through the area he loved. Thank you also to Sheila Dempster Calvert for

Acknowledgements

your emails and photos. I felt privileged to read the stories about your father that you so generously shared. What a remarkable father and grand-father he was.

Thank you to my archive researchers from all across the country and up North: Jim Bowman, Cheryl Charlie, Jodi-Ann Eskritt, Eva Holland, and Murray Peterson for finding the treasures contained in the archives. The images and archived newspaper excerpts give the story so much more depth. What an awesome team. I would also like to acknowledge the work of Shannon Olsen at the Yukon Archives for her assistance, and Tim Hersche at Depot for his keen interest in this adventure.

Thank you, Eleni Papavasiliou and Mikaela Karram, for helping out with all the computer issues, and there were many. I can't begin to imagine where I would have been without you both.

Very special thanks to my Friday morning grade seven reading and edit-ing group at Westcot Elementary School in West Vancouver. Ms. Meghan Stewart, Justine Wong, Amir Mirpourian, Iman Hassanally, Eram Lee, Shivani Mehta, Kyle Kirkwood, Chiara Crestani, Aki Ho, Rachel Kang, Nadia Chigmaroff, Saman Ghahremani, Raven Hawthorne, Esther Han, and Quinn Stevens. I will fondly remember meeting with all of you each Friday; it was a highlight in my week. Your helpful comments, eagerness, and interest in this piece of Canadian history made the writing of this book such fun.

And to Bob Cameron, author, historian, and friend. I enjoyed spending time with you in Whitehorse, and thank you for reading the manuscript and for your meaningful comments.

Thank you to Ed, Julie, David, and Christopher. Our dinner discus-sions centered on the story always gave me the boost I needed. You were with me at the Heritage Centre, Andrew's graduation, and all the way along the journey. Thank you so much. Christopher, thank you for reading each chapter and for your two thumbs up.

Thank you, Dad, for instilling in me a love of books. All the hours you spent reading to me as a child gave me the confidence to write my own words. Mom, I know you never read the entire story, but I am grateful for your support and your encouragement during the writing of the manu-script. Knowing you both will never hold this book in your hands fills my heart with sadness, but I hope you would be pleased.

To my husband Michael, and children Andrew, Victoria, Mikaela, Steve, and Kiyomi; your presence in my life is an unimaginable gift. You truly give my life meaning. I can never thank you enough for the support you showed me and for handling "life" (and there was plenty of it) while I wrote. I am so very blessed.

Introduction

My son Andrew was graduating from the Royal Canadian Mounted Police Academy, known as Depot,[1] in Regina, Saskatchewan, on May 28, 2010. Andrew is the second member of our family to become a Mountie. My grandfather, Andrew D. Cruickshank, was the first, and he patrolled the far reaches of the Canadian North in the 1920s.

Old red-brick buildings line the roads within Depot. All of these streets are named after fallen officers of the Royal Canadian Mounted Police, the Royal Northwest Mounted Police, and the North West Mounted Police force that preceded them. On that day the magnificent apple tree that stands beside the chapel was filled with fragrant apple blossoms of springtime. The chapel, where the Sunday service was held during the graduation ceremony, is the oldest building in Regina.[2] At one side of the Parade Square is the cenotaph with the names of all who gave their lives in the line of duty, and outside the Drill Hall sits a cannon that was hauled across the Prairies during the 1874 March West made by the Dominion's first mounted police force, known as the North West Mounted Police. There, the sense of heritage permeates the setting and reaches out to all those present. This feeling of history, and, more importantly, its connection to the development of Canada, touches everyone within its confines.

Just outside the gates of Depot is the RCMP Heritage Centre, a building that houses the story of the force, its past, and its present.

Within this impressive glass, wood, and stone structure is the interactive display featuring the Lost Patrol, along with other informative records of the past.

I am a fourth generation Canadian and really knew nothing about the Lost Patrol. As I sat there, listening to the recording and looking at photos and artifacts, I was haunted by their story. Just a few hours later, Corporal Sean Chiddenton (Drill, Deportment and Tactical Unit at Depot) handed me a copy of the handwritten diary of Inspector Francis J. Fitzgerald. His comment: "You won't be able to put this down until you have read every word." He was right, and while my family ate dinner that night, I read and read. I knew I wanted to tell the story of the Lost Patrol of 1910.

This is a tragic account of four men lost in the wilds of a Yukon winter, and four others who were sent out to find them. The Winter Patrol, led by Inspector F.J. Fitzgerald, left Fort McPherson, Northwest Territories, in late December 1910, and headed for Dawson City in the Yukon Territories. Their route would take them 670 kilometres over a treacherous terrain of mountains, glaciers, and frozen riverbeds. The four men of the 1910 patrol were carrying dispatches, mail, and government excise taxes, all documents needed to secure Canadian sovereignty in the Arctic. The routine trip was expected to take thirty days.

This patrol, however, would turn out to be anything but routine, and instead would become one that made international news. *Death Wins in the Arctic* is a description of their daily struggles in the darkness of the winter season and the epic battle the men made to stay alive, as based on Fitzgerald's daily journal records of their travel. It tells of their tremendous courage, their willingness to face unthinkable conditions, and their dedication to fulfill the oath they took. The narrative continues using the daily journal written by search leader Jack Dempster, which also tells of the dedication of fellow officers who put their lives and skills to the test, as they raced against time to find the missing winter patrol lost somewhere in the unforgiving Yukon wilderness.

The Mountie is an instantly recognized symbol of Canada, yet very little is known of the lives of the individual members and their particular contributions to our history. What I found during my months of research is that the early daily reports, all handwritten by the men of the force, gives us historical information describing our country in the process of becoming a nation unique in the world. Their gift to future generations was not only to keep law and order in the development of a nation, but also to leave, in the reports, a written account of the lands they patrolled, the people they met, and the wildlife that lived in the region. Many of the early Mounties took incredible photographs that document the land and its inhabitants, thus providing us with an insightful and valuable pictorial history as well.

Death Wins in the Arctic: The Lost Winter Patrol of 1910 uses the terminology of the time. When Fitzgerald records the daily events, he is using Imperial measurements, temperatures in Fahrenheit, and distance in miles. He uses the local names for creeks and rivers. I have taken the liberty to convert temperatures into Celsius and distance into metric for today's reader but have continued to use the local names as originally recorded by the hands of both Fitzgerald and Dempster.

Their story is indeed "where legend and reality become one."[3]

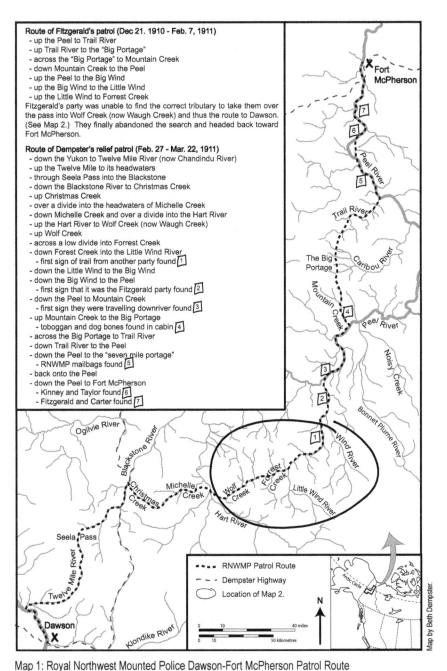

Route of Fitzgerald's patrol (Dec 21. 1910 - Feb. 7, 1911)
- up the Peel to Trail River
- up Trail River to the "Big Portage"
- across the "Big Portage" to Mountain Creek
- down Mountain Creek to the Peel
- up the Peel to the Big Wind
- up the Big Wind to the Little Wind
- up the Little Wind to Forrest Creek

Fitzgerald's party was unable to find the correct tributary to take them over the pass into Wolf Creek (now Waugh Creek) and thus the route to Dawson. (See Map 2.) They finally abandoned the search and headed back toward Fort McPherson.

Route of Dempster's relief patrol (Feb. 27 - Mar. 22, 1911)
- down the Yukon to Twelve Mile River (now Chandindu River)
- up the Twelve Mile to its headwaters
- through Seela Pass into the Blackstone
- down the Blackstone River to Christmas Creek
- up Christmas Creek
- over a divide into the headwaters of Michelle Creek
- down Michelle Creek and over a divide into the Hart River
- up the Hart River to Wolf Creek (now Waugh Creek)
- up Wolf Creek
- across a low divide into Forrest Creek
- down Forrest Creek into the Little Wind River
  - first sign of trail from another party found 1
- down the Little Wind to the Big Wind
- down the Big Wind to the Peel
  - first sign that it was the Fitzgerald party found 2
- down the Peel to Mountain Creek
  - first sign they were travelling downriver found 3
- up Mountain Creek to the Big Portage
  - toboggan and dog bones found in cabin 4
- across the Big Portage to Trail River
- down Trail River to the Peel
- down the Peel to the "seven mile portage"
  - RNWMP mailbags found 5
- back onto the Peel
- down the Peel to Fort McPherson
  - Kinney and Taylor found 6
  - Fitzgerald and Carter found 7

Map 1: Royal Northwest Mounted Police Dawson-Fort McPherson Patrol Route

Patrols along this route were still made annually until 1921, but because of the fatal trip of 1910–11, measures were taken to prevent another tragedy. Future patrols hired an Aboriginal guide, cabins were built and regular caches were established along the trail in case of food shortages, and most importantly, the Forrest Creek Trail was clearly marked so that the cut-off would not be missed again. These measures proved successful.

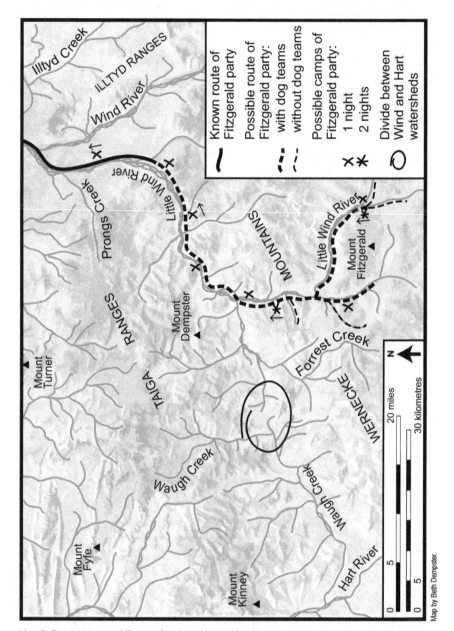

Map by Beth Dempster.

Map 2: Detailed Areas of Forrest Creek and Little Wind River

Under normal circumstances, and, if on the correct route, a patrol would spend two days to travel the sixty-five kilometre divide between the Wind and Hart river watersheds, which would then lead them on the last leg of the journey and into Dawson City. Fitzgerald and the men could not locate the Forrest Creek turn-off, and being unable to find their route forward, they had no choice but to head back to Fort McPherson.

45 Below in a.m. Tuesday Jan. 31st. 62 Below in p.m. Fine with slight
SW wind. Going heavy, travelled part of the time on our old trail, but
it was filled in. Skin peeling off our faces and parts of the body and lips
all swollen and split. I suppose this is caused by feeding on dog meat.
Everybody feeling the cold very much, for want of proper food.

— INSPECTOR FITZGERALD'S DIARY

The tree exploded and the noise cracked through the air like a gunshot. The terrifying sound echoed throughout a desolate and frozen landscape, yet the four men appeared to be deaf — no one moved a muscle. The temperature, a bone-chilling -43 degrees Celsius, had caused the veins of sap within the tree to freeze and expand and trunk to contract, splitting the bark wide open. Royal Northwest Mounted Police Inspector Francis J. Fitzgerald could only wonder: if the cold could do this to a tree, what could it be doing to the men? Immobilized by the frigid air, lightheaded, and weakened from hunger, the men just stared with empty eyes at the place where the fire had once burned.

Fitzgerald, a twenty-two-year veteran of the RNWMP and one of their most experienced men in the North, may also have wondered when things had started to go so terribly wrong.

PART ONE

---◆---

Fitzgerald:
The Winter Patrol of 1910

ONE
Tetl'it Zheh: The Story Begins

21 Below. Wednesday, Jan. 21. Strong N. wind, with heavy mist...
Left Fort McPherson at 7:45 a.m. Nooned [had lunch] *two spells up*
river [the Peel River] *and camped in Indian cabin 15 miles up river.*
Going very heavy in some places.

—INSPECTOR FITZGERALD'S DIARY

It was four days before Christmas Eve of 1910, and the men stationed at the tiny northern post of Fort McPherson in the Northwest Territories were preparing for a feast. The fort, a small settlement situated near the confluence of the Peel and Mackenzie Rivers, located just ninety-six kilometres from the edge of the Arctic Ocean, had been established as a Hudson's Bay Company (HBC) trading post in 1840. It was named after a high-ranking HBC official of the time, Murdoch McPherson, the chief factor in charge of the British-based fur-trading enterprise in the territory then known as Rupert's Land.[1]

For many years the Gwich'in, or People of the Caribou as they called themselves, had led a seasonal nomadic lifestyle, following the winter and summer hunts for caribou, walrus, seal, and a variety of fish — their source of food and other necessities of life. But their lifestyle had changed once foreign explorers, missionaries, and fur traders appeared in their land, and particularly when European manufactured goods as items for trade were introduced to their area. By now, the Gwich'in were trading beaver, fox, lynx, wolf, and martin furs exclusively with the Hudson's Bay Company in return for a variety of supplies, such as tobacco, guns, and ammunition. The people were also known as the Loucheux, the name given to them by early French missionaries.

The successful growth of the HBC post, built at the site of a Gwich'in hunting camp known locally as Tetl'it Zheh (meaning "town at the head-water") soon led to the arrival of the first Anglican missionary, Archdeacon Robert McDonald. Shortly afterwards the village acquired a post office and the Royal Northwest Mounted Police[2] established a detachment at the northerly site in 1903. Fort McPherson quickly became a thriving little community inhabited by Europeans and the Gwich'in. McDonald married a Native woman from the band and together they began to teach English to the First Nations people and translate the Bible into the Aboriginal language.

A gentle snow was falling. Someone from the tiny town had brought in black spruce boughs to decorate the RNWMP barracks. The men were preparing for Christmas. A cracking fire helped to keep the chill out and as the temperatures rose inside, the aroma of evergreens grew stronger and encouraged thoughts of Christmas. Big chunks of caribou steak were seasoned with salt and pepper. Knobby potatoes, saved for the occasion, along with rubbery carrots and greeny-white parsnips, were scrubbed and made ready for the pot. Fresh vegetables in the North during winter were unheard of, but, although advanced in age, these still would provide a mouthwatering taste of home-cooking for the men who had come from more southerly parts of the country, some even as far away as the United Kingdom. There would also be a fox stew on the menu and a platter piled high with doughy buns. A traditional Christmas pudding was a problem, but the cook did have dried fruit that could be made into something tasty.

The Gwich'in people had been invited, and would bring additional delicacies with them: dried Arctic char (a red-fleshed fish), brown trout, and possibly fish eggs mixed with dried berries. There would be cele-brating with song, drums, and dancing. A holiday feast was a much-looked-forward-to event at Fort McPherson, but Inspector Fitzgerald and his three-member patrol wouldn't be at the dining table for this

Christmas Eve dinner. Instead, they had been given orders to mush on patrol toward Dawson City, Yukon Territories. Orders had come through from A. Bowen Perry, the commissioner at the RNWMP headquarters in Regina, Saskatchewan. Earlier in the year he had sent a telegram confirming Fitzgerald's instructions to Superintendent A.E. (Arthur Edward) Snyder, the commanding officer stationed at Dawson City in the Yukon.

Royal Northwest Mounted Police, Regina, May 19, 1910

Sir,

I have the honour to inform you that I have instructed Inspector Fitzgerald to patrol from Fort McPherson to Dawson next winter. This will enable me to get into direct communication with him by telegraph. He expects to reach Dawson, 1-2-11. The usual patrol from Dawson will not be made.

I have the honour to be, sir,
Your obedient servant,
A. Bowen Perry,
Commissioner.[3]

Fort McPherson sits on a bluff overlooking the Peel River, facing the beautiful Richardson Mountains. It is the oldest of the Mackenzie Delta communities. Photo circa 1909.

Glenbow Archives NA-513-17.

It appears most likely that Fitzgerald would have received his instructions during the summer patrol of that year, when he was at either Herschel Island or Fort McPherson, both of which were under his command. But it has not been possible to confirm exactly where or when the orders came through to him. Interestingly, on April 18, 1911, Lieutenant Colonel White, the comptroller of the RNWMP was quoted as having said in Ottawa, "Inspector Fitzgerald and the three men with him [Carter, Kinney. and Taylor] were to be selected for the Mountie contingent to the coronation of King George V."[4] The coronation was to take place on June 22, 1911. Perhaps once Perry relayed his message to Fitzgerald upon the patrol's arrival in Dawson, he and the three men who had been selected to accompany him would then have made their way south to Regina ultimately to take passage on a trans-Atlantic ship scheduled to reach London in time for the coronation. The winter patrol had been busy preparing for their departure, as instructed by their commanding officer. They were to leave on the day of the winter solstice, December 21, 1910, a day when the sun would not rise above the horizon.

Herschel Island was a thriving whaling community until the early 1900s. The Pacific Steam Whaling Company depleted the bowhead whale, prized for its baleen, the flexible material found in the whale's mouth, which was used for the "bones" in the corsets of fashionable European women.

Northern winter patrols were a central part of the Mounties' role. The most important things they carried on their sleds were small canvas bags, each the size of a backpack, inscribed with the letters RNWMP. After many weeks, the government documents carried in the travel-worn bags would end up in Ottawa. The various bags contained, among other things, official reports from Fort McPherson and other northern RNWMP posts, such as those at Herschel Island, Dawson City, and Forty Mile (a day's dogsled travel outside Dawson City), and customs duties collected from the captains of American whaling ships that hunted the bowhead and the right or baleen whale in the Beaufort Sea. The mailbags also held letters that would be delivered to the Mounties' families who lived in more southerly locations, far away from the isolated detachments in the North — families who could scarcely imagine the world their sons and brothers inhabited.

The arrival of mail in the early 1900s was an event greeted with much hope and anticipation at both the lonely northern detachments and the more southerly homes, but a post office held a special significance in the North where life was so isolated. Not only was it a place where mail was delivered and collected, but, as a government office, it also established the sovereignty of the Dominion in an area so recently overrun with American gold miners, whalers, and even explorers from other parts of the world who wanted to claim Canada's Arctic as their own. In 1910, Canada's control over this area could not be taken for granted.

The patrols also had another purpose. They established the visible presence of the RNWMP sent there to preserve the laws of the Dominion. The Mounties were protectors, helpers, counsellors, and even physicians. They recorded details of life in the North, documented events as they travelled from settlement to settlement, and also observed the migratory movements of wild game, particularly the caribou. Their observations made them early historians of the young Canada and the first conservation officers in the land.

Northern winter days in Fort McPherson were experienced as a hazy dusky twilight. In 1910, from December 21st to the 27th, the sun did not break the horizon, and the inhabitants of the territory received only twilight from 11:10 a.m. until 4:44 p.m. From the 28th there would be an half hour of sunlight from 1:45 p.m. to 2:15 p.m., and each day from then on, the daylight would increase by about nine minutes until reaching the longest day of the year. During the dark cold winter months of snow and ice, travel was done using dog teams. Toboggan-type sleds, made and sold by First Nations people, were the favoured mode of transportation. But supplying toboggans were not the only way the Aboriginal people assisted the RNWMP. For the Europeans, finding their way through dark forests and along many-forked waterways during the shadowy days of winter was a daunting task.

Native guides were needed to accompany the patrols. The indigenous people knew the trails and frozen riverbeds and could easily find their way around. Their skills were born of the harsh environment that was their home. Even the children learned how to observe and interpret their surroundings. Elders told them stories that not only helped pass the long winter nights, but imparted knowledge of hunting skills, wildlife habits, and the geography of their land needed for survival. Expert at tracking, the Native guide would also supplement food supplies for the travelling patrols by tracking moose, caribou, or fox, and snaring ptarmigan.

Glenbow Archives, NA-513-24.

Loads are securely lashed to the birchbark toboggans, and members of the small community stand together with the officers who are about to leave from Fort McPherson for a winter patrol. Though not a photo of Fitzgerald and his men, it does demonstrate the closeness of the community members and the tradition of a send off for members of the RNWMP.

For some reason, in that winter of 1910, there would be no First Nations guide accompanying the four officers of the winter patrol. Jimmie Husky, of the Gwich'in First Nations, who had been on a previous Dawson to Fort McPherson patrol, had turned down the request to go along. To this day, the reason for his refusal remains an unanswered question. Two other Natives had offered to go instead, but Fitzgerald, for some reason, had said no.

It was in the chilly Arctic dawn of December 21, 1910, that Fitzgerald ordered the paws of each dog to be checked. All the RNWMP dogs from Fort McPherson would be making the patrol to Dawson City. The inspector's own dogs had come with him from Herschel Island and were all in good condition to travel, with the exception of "Bob," who had sustained an injury when coming across the frozen Arctic Ocean. Bob was left behind at the fort.

Each of the men loaded their personal kits aboard the three sleds. Their trail clothes were basic. They would wear long woollen underwear and woollen pants. They packed a few woollen shirts and a duck-down parka that reached the knees, complete with a fur-lined hood. This, the only jacket the men had, was to serve as a windbreaker as well. Scratchy piles of wool socks filled out their bags, as did mukluks, moccasins, and fur-lined gloves to protect their hands from the freezing air. The men, summoning all their power to live under the weight of their garments and in the face of the northern elements, would run alongside the toboggans, taking turns for a well-deserved rest in a sled, when needed. The trailblazer, sent out in front of the running dogs, would be wearing snowshoes as he established the trail for the rest to follow. Only the fit could endure the rigorous demands of winter patrols.

Fitzgerald walked around the three sleds, one at a time, to make sure that all the cargo, including personal gear, official documents, and food supplies, was lashed securely. This patrol would be the seventh of its kind. However, in all previous patrols, the route had been in the other direction, travelling from Dawson City in the Yukon to Fort McPherson, Northwest Territories. This time the route was in reverse, from Fort McPherson to Dawson. This is a significant difference since it was impossible to get the same quantity and quality of provisions to supply the outgoing patrol in the more northern Fort McPherson than could be obtained in Dawson City. The trip, covering a distance of 670 kilometres, was expected to take about thirty days, with their expected arrival in Dawson to be close to the end of January. They carried barely enough food for this period of time, and were planning to shoot large wild game to supplement their food supply as they travelled along the trail, a traditional route established by the Gwich'in people.

The bulging loads were piled high and carried 817 kilograms of food and gear, equally divided among the three sleds. The inventory, which was protected by a heavy tarp, included: 408 kilograms of dried fish for the dog food, thirty-four kilograms of bacon, four-and-a-half kilograms of corned beef, six kilograms of lard, four-and-a-half kilograms of butter, one kilogram of salt, eight kilograms of tinned milk, fifty-four kilograms of flour, six-and-a-half kilograms of dried fruit, thirteen kilograms of precooked and frozen beans, eight kilograms of coffee and tea, thirteen kilograms of tobacco, sixteen kilograms of sugar, and three kilograms of baking powder. They also had nine kilograms of candles, one .30-.30 carbine (a light rifle, suitable only for hunting large game), two axes, a pocket barometer, matches, watches, a camp stove, and tent, as well as the important documents held in the mail and dispatch bags. For warmth at night, each man had an Alaskan down-filled sleeping blanket.

Accompanying Inspector Fitzgerald were forty-one-year-old Special Constable Sam Carter, who would be the patrol guide. Carter, a twenty-two-year veteran of the force, had previously been on patrol four years earlier, but from Dawson City to Fort McPherson. Constable Richard O'Hara Taylor, from Scotland, had joined the Mounties in 1905 and was just a year older than twenty-seven-year-old Constable George Francis Kinney, an American who had been a member for three years. This would be the first patrol for both Kinney and Taylor, and they were packed and eager for the journey. Their leader, Francis Fitzgerald, known as the Mounties' "Northern Man,"[5] had much experience with patrols.

Outside the Hudson's Bay post, the dogs, also anxious to get on the trail, growled and yipped. Their barks filled the air, causing the well-wishers to gather in front of the detachment. Goodbyes were shouted over the din, and at 7:45 a.m. on Wednesday, December 21, 1910, the mushers called to the dogs and they were off into the white-covered wilderness. With the departure of the winter patrol, Corporal Somers and Constable Blake were left in charge in charge of the RNWMP post. Little did they know that they would never see their colleagues alive again.

With only three sleds and four men, one of the officers, possibly Carter initially, since he was the patrol guide, had gone out ahead to break the trail. Each man would take his turn as trailblazer. With the newly fallen granular snow, the dogs would struggle and be unable to gain footing unless a man on snowshoes helped to tamp down the surface.

Before long, a mist arose from the nearby Peel River, and, with a southeast wind blowing, the area soon became thick with moist air. Dim light and foggy conditions made the travel treacherous. Sounds became muffled. The panting of the dogs, the soft plopping of the snow falling from the branches, and the rasping sound of the sled runners on the wet surface made it difficult to tell whether the sounds were in front or behind them. The scenario almost created a sensation of an unknown force stalking them. The scrawny black spruce lining the trail tilted and leaned at alarming angles, their scraggly fog-laden branches seeming to clutch at anything that passed, threatening to halt any forward movement. Was this eerie setting of the Winter Solstice an omen of things to come?

Glenbow Archives, PD-383-2-13.

The first step at a lunch stop was to always put each toboggan on its side so that the dogs could not dash off into the wilderness without their master in control. With the sled tipped, the dogs would not try and pull, but instead would lie down and rest after being given water to drink.

Fitzgerald called a stop at noon. It was midday and the pervasive gloomy darkness had made travelling tough. A rest break for some sustenance was needed. The first day's lunch of beans and tea helped give the men renewed energy, and, after finishing their hot drink and righting the sleds, they were off into the gloom once more. The going became tougher. At intervals the trailblazer would yell aloud and the man by the sleds would call back. They did this every few minutes. Not to do so meant running the risk of the man in front being lost or their sleds being separated in the dusky light.

As the dimness was beginning to edge into total darkness, they came across an abandoned Aboriginal cabin. Fitzgerald decided their first night out on the trail would be spent there. The structure, though dilapidated, would also save them time that night. With no need to set up a tent, they would have fewer chores by simply camping overnight inside the four walls and would also have a head start for their departure in the morning.

In what would become a nightly ritual, the four men first tended to the dogs, checking paws for signs of injury, and feeding them before attending to their personal needs. These fifteen dogs were a lifeline for the men on patrol. For now, they would pull the sleds over the divide created by the Richardson and the Ogilvie Mountains, as the men made their way south to Dawson City. Making sure the dogs were well fed and safe was important. Even a small injury could lead to disaster. At night each dog was tied to a tree with a carefully measured length of chain, to make sure that one animal could not reach the other. Being a dog-wolf mix, these animals were athletic and strong, but still had that wild instinct and one could easily attack another as food was being dished out. The threat of a wolf attack presented another nightly concern. Many packs of Yukon wolves roamed the area and were known to have attacked dogs at the encampments.

The huskies were fed a meal of dried fish, and, after some snow and ice were melted on the camp stove and cooled, they were given water to drink. It wasn't long before the dogs, one by one, made a circle in the snow at the base of its tree, and formed a "bed." Soon all went to sleep, curled up with noses tucked in under tails. Their heavy coats would keep them warm during the night as the temperatures plummeted even farther and the wind picked up.

Working quickly that first night, the men unloaded their gear and took what they needed into the cabin. Heading back outside, they chopped down spruce boughs with their axes, bringing them into the cabin and laying them out on the floor. One of the men had stayed inside and began to cook a meal of bacon on the camp stove. Soon the aroma of sizzling strips filled the small abode, likely causing empty stomachs to growl. The cook made bannock by mixing flour and baking powder with a little water, and created a simple "oven" for baking the bread by placing one frying pan over the other. The hot bannock soaked up the bacon grease, creating a salty flavour much enjoyed by the men.

Dishwashing required more ice to be melted. Once dinner was cleaned up, the men relaxed by candlelight. Water was boiled for tea, and tobacco tamped into pipes. As the candlelight flames flickered, shadows moved along the walls.

A wolf howled somewhere in the distance, and one of the dogs responded. Wolves generally howl during the evening hours and at early dawn, when they are on the hunt. Sometimes the howling is to attract a mate, but they frequently howl in a group, a tactic designed to help protect the pack. Each wolf has its own pitch or coding, often determined by the size and the health of the animal, so when many join together, they can trick another pack into thinking there are more wolves present, warning outsiders to stay away.[6]

Seconds later the rest of the dogs raised their heads and answered the ancestral call.

TWO
Evenings of Storytelling

With trappers, whalers and prospectors pouring into Canada's north, the North-West Mounted Police were sent to the newest frontier to carry out patrols, to protect indigenous peoples and to enforce laws. The Dominion used the force's presence to claim Canada's sovereignty. These men endured tough and dangerous conditions.[1]

As the evening hours passed, a smoky haze gathered below the wooden slats of the roof. Tobacco smoke, mixed with heat from the camp stove and the smells of dinner, made the cabin quite comfortable and cozy. Every now and then, however, a blast of freezing air pushed in through the chinks in the walls, reminding the four men that they were on the trail and not in their detachment at Fort McPherson. Junior officers Kinney and Taylor were pleased to be in experienced company and keen to hear firsthand the stories of the beginnings of the mounted force. Kinney, being an American, had a special interest in the "March West," as it was called, of the North West Mounted Police and asked Fitzgerald to retell the story. A long night lay ahead of them, and so Fitzgerald, drawing on his pipe, relaxed, and began to speak.

It was because of the Yankee "free traders" and their encroaching on Canadian territory and mistreatment of the Indians that led to our first prime minister, Sir John A. Macdonald, forming the North West Mounted Police in 1873.[2] The brazen free traders were American whisky outlaws. Even though they knew their actions were illegal, they smuggled alcohol from Montana across the border into the area then known as the Northwest Territories. Their goal: to get cheap furs from the Indians. With no police force or army on the vast expanse of the Canadian prairies at the time, the area was wide open to any type of endeavour, legal or not. Men did as they pleased, and in so doing created a major problem for our prime minister. But he was not to be outdone. Macdonald's solution was a unique system of law enforcement — create a police force on horseback. Once he had assembled a mounted force, he would organize a march west and bring law and order to the Canadian Prairies.

Ottawa had not only received word that Native peace was being destroyed, but that smallpox, brought by these traders, was killing the First Nations population.[3] But it wasn't just smallpox that caused the deaths. Excessive alcohol consumption, whisky in particular, was the villain. In one winter alone, more than seventy Blackfoot First Nations men and women died or were killed as a result of alcohol poisoning or drunkenness. During the same period, a group of American men shot and killed thirty children and women of the Assiniboine First Nations in Cypress Hills, in southern Saskatchewan.

It was a bloody massacre stemming from the "firewater," as the Indians called alcohol. A group of Montana free traders accused members of the Assiniboine people of horse theft — a claim that led to a deadly battle in 1873.[4] Once the first shot was fired, their warriors sent a volley of arrows into the sky, but these were no match for the hail of bullets from the American Henry and Winchester repeaters. Booze-fuelled outlaws bludgeoned helpless victims and decapitated an elderly Indian named Wankantu and stuck his head on a spike outside the fort. The rest, left to rot in the heat of the day, became easy carrion for scavengers.[5] Macdonald was outraged.

Still the free traders extended their illegal commerce with the Indians on the Prairies and continued to use the frontier-trading forts they had built along the border in an area known as the Saskatchewan Valley as their headquarters. The Aboriginal people went there to exchange their furs for other goods, principally alcohol. One buffalo hide, brought to an opening cut into the palisade, bought two tin cups of firewater and the potential destruction of the Aboriginal way of life.

These forts had names such as Slide Out, Kipp, and Standoff, but the most notorious and corrupt was Fort Whoop-Up. It was named after the firewater, or, as the traders put it, "Whoop-up juice" — a boiled-down concoction of tobacco juice (sometimes from the spittoon), Jamaican ginger, raw high-proof alcohol, molasses, and water. Deadly stuff! This notorious fort would be the first destination for the new North West Mounted Police. Originally named Fort Hamilton after a mercantile firm in Montana, the fort was built in 1869 near the junction of the Oldman and the St. Mary Rivers. It became the American trade headquarters on the southwestern prairie frontier where the Indians would bring buffalo hides and other furs such as wolf, for trading.[6] It became so popular that by 1873, the Hudson's Bay Company had lost most of the business from the Blackfoot tribe to the free traders.

When the British North American Act was passed in 1876, the government undertook the responsibility of the First Nations people, and the NWMP were sent to protect them from the destructive whisky trade. Here, a family of the Blood Nation huddles outside the palisade walls of "Fort Whoop-Up."

Glenbow Archives, NA-550-18.

The force Macdonald intended to create would become the law of the land and put an end to the illegal whisky trade at these forts and bring the free traders to justice. This would be no ordinary police unit but instead would be modelled after the Irish Constabulary.[7] He began preparing for such a force of two hundred men in the winter of 1869–70. In fact, his plan was part of Canada's preparation to take control over lands that the Hudson's Bay Company was selling to the government.[8] These men would have the customs, traditions, and practices of an army, yet the officers chosen would have civil and government duties as well as general police duties. Macdonald wanted a centrally controlled police force, a corps of mounted riflemen able to respond quickly to disputes anywhere in the West. They would enforce law and root out corruption.[9] The men would wear scarlet coats to resemble those British military officers who had come to Canada during the War of 1812 and built up a respectful relationship with the Indian people.

After the newly formed force had been assembled at Fort Dufferin, in Manitoba near Winnipeg, and with Commissioner George French as their leader, they prepared for what would become the infamous "March West" through the "Great Lone Land."[10] On July 8, 1874, the three hundred members of the North West Mounted Police — the youngest was the bugle boy, Fred Bagley, age fifteen — dressed in their scarlet jackets, left the fort heading west towards the Rocky Mountains. They had 339 horses, 142 oxen, 114 Red River carts, seventy-three wagons, and two cannons, each of which weighed a ton. These cannons were to be used to demolish the walls of the palisaded frontier forts. A 1,300-kilometre journey lay ahead of them. During this epic trek, the men had to be self-sufficient, and even though they carried an enormous amount of supplies, these would prove to be woefully inadequate.

The monumental undertaking would take over ninety days. The Mounties rode or walked alongside their horses, with oxen dragging the cannons, during what became a most daunting journey. Gopher holes pitted the arid plains, and the horses stumbled and tripped as they hauled the carts with supplies. During some days torrential downpours turned the prairie dust to mud flats and they were mired in muck, everything absolutely sodden. And if the rains were not enough, frequent thunderstorms plagued the march. On the open prairie, with no shelter, they were totally exposed to lightening strikes, but miraculously, no one was struck. Both men and animals often travelled for days without proper food or water and what water they did drink was often contaminated — leading to violent bouts of diarrhea. Most of the horses died of starvation and exhaustion along the route.

NORTH WEST MOUNTED POLICE.

———•◦•———

150 additional Constables and Sub-Constables being required for the above Force, the following information is published for the guidance of those desirous of joining the Force :—

(1).—Candidates must be active, able-bodied men of thoroughly sound constitution and exemplary character. They should be able to ride well, and to read and write either the English or French language.

(2).—The term of engagement is three years.

(3).—The rates of payments are as follow :—

> *Constables ·············$1 per diem.*
> *Sub-Constables········· 75 c. "*

with free rations ; a free kit on joining ; clothing ; boots ; quarters ; fuel ; and light ; and the Government is empowered to give a free grant of 160 acres of land to all well-conducted men on completion of three years' service.

(4.)—All transport expenses of those who are approved and accepted for service will be borne by the Government.

(5).—The undersigned will attend at

Glenbow Archives, NA-2706-1.

The North West Mounted Police was formed in 1873. The enrolment advertising attracted men from Canada, Great Britain, Australia, and the United States.

And the insects — those thousands of insects — were another source of torment. Mosquitoes, beyond what could possibly be imagined, attacked man and beast alike.

The air was described as being black with the voracious pests and the men were bitten unmercifully. The high-pitched whine nearly drove them mad.

———◆———

Fitzgerald paused to quote one of the members of the march, a Henri Julien, who had written in his diary "all agreed that nowhere had they seen anything equal to the mosquitoes of the prairie…. [They] rise in columns out of the spongy soil under our feet and do regular battle with us."[11] His three companions urged him to continue, and as the evening passed the story continued to unfold.

———◆———

Some days weather and insects combined forces. Tents blew down in the blasting hail and windstorms, and during one such storm the sound of the hail slamming into the tents gradually took on an unsettling sound. Looking outside, the men saw the hailstones had ceased and locusts were falling from the sky.

Clouds of the huge grasshoppers billowed from the west, with "prismatic colors of the sun's rays glistening off their vibrating wings."[12] The noise was deafening. One swarm was estimated as being 2,896 kilometres long and perhaps 177 kilometres wide, containing an estimated ten billion insects. The mass took five days to pass, eating leather, canvas, the fodder for the animals, and handles of wooden tools as they made their way.[13] Orders were shouted to dismantle the tents. With each step taken by the men a sickening crunch reached their ears. Squashed hoppers made the ground as slippery as if they were trying to stand on ice. They broke camp in record speed to save what they could. Their situation was desperate and yet even this did not stop them. The men carried on, determined to put an end to the unrest in the prairies, and they endured all this for just 75 cents per day.[14]

Just 320 kilometres into their 1,300-kilometre journey, the deaths of the horses turned the mounted force into foot soldiers.[15] At this point, the chances of making it to the Prairies seemed slim, but their fortunes were about to change. In an extraordinary turn of events, the bedraggled force met an ally who would become their salvation in bringing stability to the West. A guide named Jerry Potts,[16] led the Mounties to Fort Whoop-Up.

Jerry Potts was adopted by an American Fur Company trader Andrew Dawson who taught Potts to read and write. In Potts's later teen years, Dawson encouraged his son to join his mother's tribe, and it was through the exposure to both cultures that Potts learned the ways of both cultures, which facilitated the peaceful relations with the NWMP and the First Nations.

Commissioner French had the wisdom to hire Potts as a scout and interpreter and in the years to come he would prove to be invaluable to the
NWMP. Potts's ability to build trust between people was a key reason why
the new Mounties were able to build a strong relationship with the local
Indian bands.

Jerry Potts, also known as Ky-yo-kosi (meaning Bear Child), was the
son of a Blood Indian woman named Namo-pisi and a Scotsman named
Andrew Potts, who had come to Canada as a clerk in the fur trade. The
boy learned the ways of both the settlers and Natives from his parents, and
during his life he had to prove to both his Indian family and white people
that he could cope with the different cultures. He learned the importance of
friendly relations and the distinct customs and etiquette of both. However,
after his father was shot dead during a fight, Namo-pisi gave him up to a
white family, and rejoined her tribe.

Potts was thirty-three years old when he met the NWMP at Fort Benton
in Montana. From then on he was their guide, scout, and interpreter, sharing
his considerable skills and detailed knowledge of the terrain of the territory
with the Mounties. For this he earned $90 per month, which was almost
three times what NWMP Constables were earning. From the time of their
arrival at Fort Whoop-Up onward, the NWMP worked closely with the
Aboriginal people of Canada, the ones they were sent out to protect, and
Jerry Potts became a very important person in the negotiations of peace
among various Indian groups living on the Prairies, on both sides of the
border. His natural ability as a peacekeeper led to their chiefs becoming solid
true allies with the North West Mounted Police — a truly amazing man.

Chief Red Crow, of the Crowfoot Nation, summed up the relationship
when he said of the Mounties, "Bad men and whiskey were killing us all so
fast that very few, indeed, of us would have been left today. The Police have
protected us as the feathers of the bird protect it from the frosts of winter.
I wish them all good, and trust that all our hearts will increase in goodness
from this time forward...."[17] The March, despite its almost overwhelming
difficulties, was a resounding success — only one officer did not survive
the ordeal — and law and order was restored. The North West Mounted
Police had fulfilled the orders given to them, but they could not have done
it without Jerry Potts.

And with that, Fitzgerald concluded his story, deep in thought. He had a common bond with Jerry Potts. Like Potts, Fitzgerald knew firsthand of the difficulties faced by a child of mixed parentage. He had left not only his Arctic detachment on December 21, but also left behind his common-law wife Lena Oonalina, an Inuit woman, and their infant daughter Annie who had been born in 1909. He had requested permission from his RNWMP superiors to marry Lena, but had been turned down.[18] He may have hoped that Annie's life would be one in which she would work to foster the bond between the Arctic Aboriginal people and the Europeans coming into their lands, gaining respect from all, just as Jerry Potts had done.

Musing on the early history of the force, the men chewed on some dried fruit and decided to call it a night, glad to be in the frigid North, rather than on the bug-infested prairies. The last of the candles had nearly sputtered out and it would be an early rise the next day. The heavy wet spruce branches cut down and brought into the cabin to help soften (and cushion) the hard floor, had now dried out and were arranged as beds and down-filled sleeping rolls were placed on top. A howling wind increased in ferocity and the fine snow found its way inside, settling in patches on the floor. Aching muscles began to relax and snores soon filled the room.

18 BELOW. THURSDAY, DEC. 22ND. STRONG S. WIND, WITH HEAVY MIST.

It was pitch black outside when the men awoke to the shrill of their alarm clock. Fitzgerald, Carter, Kinney, and Taylor stretched and extracted themselves from their warm sleeping rolls. Each had a morning duty, and thus began their day. The most important job was to tend to the dogs. The cabin door cracked and groaned as they pushed it open. Snow had collected and partially sealed the door shut, and after one final heave a dreadful cold gusted into the cabin.

Kinney was aghast. More snow had fallen during the night and the dogs were gone. Had the men slept through a wolf raid? Hoping against hope, he whistled. A few seconds later, and to his immense relief, one furry head popped up out of the snow, then another, and another. Barks greeted their master and before long each dog had shaken off the fresh powder, was stretching and yawning, just as the men had done. Wagging tails sent snow flying like a blizzard. Dried fish was divided among the hungry canines and water dished out. The dogs would have some time to digest their food before being hitched in teams and set to work.

Now it was the men's turn to prepare for the day. After devouring bannock and scalding coffee, each man shook out his sleeping blanket, then rolled it up and stuffed it into his kit. Once the gear and camp stove were packed in the toboggans, and the spruce boughs returned outside, the dogs were brought to the line, one by one. Keen to go, they jumped and danced in the snow as they eagerly awaited their turn.

As before, one man set off out front to pack down the trail. It would be a welcome relief if the patrol could find a hunter's trail, but none had been found so far. Had they been doing the patrol in the reverse direction, from Dawson City to Fort McPherson, a horse and sled carrying the supplies would have broken the first eighty to110 kilometres. A broken trail would have allowed them time to get their "trail legs" before the harsher slogging of making their own way began. But this was not to be for Fitzgerald's patrol; they would be breaking trail along the contours of the Peel River on their own. It was going to be tough going, and, with the wind chill, the temperature was around -45°C. When a sufficient time had passed for the trailblazer to make the opening stretch of the trail passable, the drivers called "mush," and the teams were off.

Carter's plan for the second day was to reach the start of a small portage, where they would leave the Peel to cut off a lengthy meander then rejoin the river again. A thick curtain of mist rose and seemed to fill every space around them, making it difficult to see and breathe with ease. Around noon, they stopped for an hour to tend to the dogs and eat some lunch themselves. The afternoon going became easier as the surface of the snow became firmer, however, the dogs were tiring and so were the men, and their eyes were sore from the strain of peering through the almost frozen mist. When they reached the entry to the portage, their goal for the day, they decided to set up at their nightly stop. Almost thirty kilometres had been covered — a good distance for a day's travel. If they continued at this rate, they might even make a record time for the patrol.

On this, their second night, they would be making camp in the open and in near darkness. As always, the task of tending the dogs was first. After each had been chained to a tree, paws were checked for signs of injury or packed ice. Next the gear was unpacked. This time the men would be sleeping in a tent, which meant that setting up the camp site would require additional time and effort. One man would make the fire, after chopping wood and using any deadfall he could find, then begin food preparations, while the other two sought out some of the slender black-spruce trunks for the tent poles and spruce boughs for their beds. The fourth would be still tending to the dogs.

After finding suitable trees for the poles, an officer felled them with a sharpened axe and stripped off the branches to provide a "soft" surface for sleeping. A considerable amount of additional wood was needed for the fire, since it would be piled high to burn all night, thus they took turns chopping. The fire was essential to their well-being. Not only would it help to generate warmth and be used for cooking, it would also help to keep predators away.

One last chore was to inspect the toboggans and scrape off any ice buildup. This meant that each night the loads would be removed from the sleds and replaced the following morning. Since the patrol was just two days into their journey, their snowshoes were in still in good condition, but repairs would be an added task as the days on the trail wore on.

Supper smells soon filled the frigid air. The coffee pot, kept heated over the open flames, was ready and the hot liquid would help to warm their bodies. The pot of beans and corned beef bubbled in an iron pot hung over the flames. Its hearty aroma caused the dogs, which were not yet settled, to bark and pull at their chains in anticipation of more food.

Once the meal was ready, the men dished their dinner onto tin plates, poured strong coffee into metal mugs, opened a can of milk, and sweetened their hot drink with sugar. The steamy food and drink cooled quickly, so conversation took second place to enjoying their meal. Just sitting by the heat of the fire and eating was a welcome respite. The fresh air and hard work of the day had made them very hungry. Dried fruit was dessert, and more ice was added to the pot of coffee, which was boiled again. At this point, they lit their pipes and started to chat.

Now Fitzgerald could continue his storytelling. Tonight's tale would recount the expanding role of the North West Mounted Police.

———————◆———————

Once the March West had successfully expelled the illegal whisky trade, the orders of the North West Mounted Police were to establish temporary detachments or camps where needed. In 1884, five hundred police officers, stationed in about forty detachments, were responsible for maintaining the law in an enormous area of over 518,000 square kilometres. As the years passed, the number of posts grew, and most of these were built in areas close to the border with the United States as a deterrent against liquor smuggling, horse theft, and other unlawful activity. Just five years later, by the end of 1899, there were about ninety detachments in strategic places across the Western Prairies.[19] The scattered locations of the detachments led to the creation of patrols, some of which were made daily or sometimes weekly. Their vigilant activity helped to create the Canada of today.

As one NWMP commissioner stationed in Regina, Lawrence Herchmer, stated: "[I]t was important not only that the police be seen, but that they also participate, individually and collectively, in the transformation of western Canada."[20] In 1890 alone, twenty years prior to the Fort McPherson patrol, the mounted policemen posted in the Prairies had travelled close to 2.4 million kilometres on patrol in that one year.[21] Officers of the "E" Division in Calgary, made 2,066 patrols in 1889, and covered over 257,600 kilometres — incredible accomplishments!

All these patrols were done on horseback, with horses often travelling a staggering distance of almost 5,000 kilometres in a single year. The following years saw an increase in the number of patrols and with that came an increase in kilometres covered. The new settlers and their police worked hard to build a new land, and one that within a few decades would carve a unique identity in the world. Patrols were done year-round, and the springtime patrols were just as difficult as those in the winter because of raging rivers swollen with winter snow and ice runoff.

Sadly, on occasion the lives of both officers and horses were claimed. One lost soul was Constable James Herron who left the NWMP Kipp detachment, a former free trader fort in what is now Alberta, on March 2, 1891. He set out alone, contrary to regulations, and was found frozen to death, two days later. Patrols were never easy. Each had to be well planned, but that still did not prevent the deaths of officers doing their duty.

Important relationships with settlers and Indians were created during the patrols. The NWMP were held in high regard, not only because they enforced the law, but also because they helped the newcomers build a life in this new country. Officers also assisted in the developing towns. They would be guards at the banks, transport people from one area to another, and share communication from one settlement to another, like information on crop successes, disasters, or weather patterns. They regularly visited the new Canadians on ranches and the homesteads that were great distances apart, helping to create a sense of community. Commissioner Herchmer was convinced that the patrols played a vital role in the settlement of the West, and in his opinion, those in the Arctic were just as crucial as the ones that began on the Prairies.

———————◆———————

The men of this patrol perched on the newly cut logs, enjoying the last bit of comfort from their tobacco and coffee. The flames shot sparks into the blackness, but within seconds the Arctic air sucked the life out of the tiny embers and billows of smoke from the green wood and spruce needles filled the air. The fire pit, piled high with black spruce logs and encouraged back to life by the brittle deadfall scrounged from under the trees, soon had the flames reaching higher into the night sky. Warmth generated near the fire caused them to become sleepy.

As the men crawled into their tent for the night, they found their shelter freezing cold, but they were tired. Once they were inside their down-filled blankets, sleep came quickly. Wood had been piled high on the fire and would be good for some time. When it went out, it went out.

THREE
Lost and Found

The lonely sunsets flame and die;
The giant valleys gulp the night;
The monster mountains scrape the sky,
Where eager stars are diamond-bright.[1]

15 BELOW. FRIDAY, DEC. 23RD. SLIGHT N.E. WIND WITH HEAVY MIST.

The tedious morning schedule began and there wasn't much talking as the men went about their chores. Richard Taylor had been assigned dog duty, and again these animals were the priority. The dogs leaped and pulled at their chains, rocking the tree trunks, sending snow falling to the earth in soft thuds from the branches above. Excitedly, they snapped at the tumbling snow. Rough pink tongues hung out of their open mouths and white clouds of breath came out in steamy puffs. Taylor grinned and scratched the lead dog's velvet ears, sending her into a delighted wiggling mass of damp fur. It was okay to show affection while the dogs were on their chains, but not during their work time. Morning was the time for the officers to thank these dedicated huskies. Even at this early stage in their journey, bonds between humans and canines were beginning to form. The dogs jumped about, causing the remainder of the snow on the branches to plop onto his head. They were hyper, hungry, and wanted their food *now*. Taylor tossed dried fish to each and brought melted snow-water for them to drink. The fish, dried the previous season, was a highly nutritious and energy-packed food, but building up enough supply to last the hard-working dogs for a year was a time-consuming task.

During the summer fish run, a "fish cache" of logs was made ready. For hundreds of years First Nations people had raised such a structure. Logs had to be notched out and stacked as if building the walls of a cabin, to a height of about 1.5 metres. More logs were then laid across the top, parallel to each other. A slash was cut through the tail of each fish and the fish were then threaded onto a thin wooden rod. These rods were suspended in the log cache, allowing air to circulate around the drying fish. Preserving food during the summer months was important to keep a substantial food supply for the RNWMP dogs — for any of the sled dogs, for that matter.

For a short while, all Richard Taylor could hear was the sounds of the chomping on dried fish. But it didn't last long. The dogs were healthy and had good appetites during this early part of the trip. It was essential to keep them that way. Every dog had its role within the unit. The lead was the heart of its team and usually is the largest and most intelligent of the pack. This dog bore the brunt of the weight for the team, and required the most time to recover from a day of pulling. The wheel dog, positioned nearest the sled, was also a very strong dog, and it was this dog's job to keep the sled straight, no matter how rough and twisted the trail. Behind the lead dog, the swing dogs added pulling power.[2] As was the RNWMP practice during a winter patrol, there was a total of fifteen dogs, five per sled.

By 7:30 a.m., with both men and dogs fed, the tent, stove, and gear packed and strapped to the toboggans, they were ready to begin day three. The plan was to mush at least thirty kilometres, and they had to get going before the cold immobilized them. It was well known that physical activity was critical in keeping blood circulating and to avoid hypothermia. The dogs were hitched in position in record time. With their muscles tense with anticipation, they leapt forward at the command "Mush!" The patrol was off again, pulling in the semi-darkness; the sun would not rise above the horizon on this day. The surface of the snow was crusty, a hard layer formed from the combination of the subzero temperatures and the wind. The trailblazer was running to make sure he kept in the lead. Providing the best footing for the dogs would prevent them from tiring too early. Without them, travel would be impossible.

The eleven-kilometre portage that would take them back to the Peel River was tough slogging. Snow from the previous night made it difficult to gain footing. Both dogs and men struggled with each step; breathing became laboured. Finally, the patrol took a break for lunch. Once they had eaten, the men continued the task of helping the dogs through the snow, pulling and pushing the sleds in an attempt to help with traction. Shouts of encouragement filled the air. However, after twenty-seven kilometres they could go no further and dropped to their knees in sheer fatigue.

The exhausted group tended to the dogs and set up camp as quickly as they could manage. Once the huskies were fed, they gathered deadfall and chopped wood. A fire was lit, the tent raised, food made and dished out, dishes were cleaned, and more wood was chopped and added to the fire. The bone-weary men, exhausted from the exertion of the day and heat of the fire, crawled into the tent for some well-deserved sleep. It didn't matter that it was still early in the evening. While the men slept, more snow fell. This unnamed place had loneliness and desolation about it, and, with the settling snow, came a great stillness.

17 BELOW. SATURDAY, DEC. 24TH. FINE, WITH STRONG S.E. WIND.

It was Christmas Eve, and the men awoke to a massive buildup of snow, a sight that filled the patrol with dismay. The travel would be even tougher than the day before. It was dark as they started out, at 8:00 a.m. They were headed south, meeting the wind head-on. Snow swirled around them, creating an even whiter cold world that was not kind to the Mounties. Sled runners sank in the deep snow, and the dogs struggled to gain their footing as they strained to move the heavy toboggans. The cold would have been torture enough, but the real nightmare was the effort it took to place one foot — or one paw — in front of the other.

A few hours later the patrol passed Colin Vitisk's place. Both the man and his shelter were known to the Mounties. This was one of the many cabins found throughout the wilds of the Yukon and were often located beside a river or along a trail. During the dark cold winter months when trapping was difficult or prospecting not feasible, the buildings were often left empty. It was accepted that anyone passing who needed a place to stay was welcome, provided the cabin was left in the condition it was found. The men of the patrol knew Vitisk, and it would have been a welcome relief had he been there, but sadly he was not. They decided not to stop for lunch, but instead kept going for another hour. Not only did the patrol pass cabins en route, they also frequently came across letters, visibly placed for pick-up by any persons passing through on their way to Dawson City. After quickly grabbing the messages, the patrol added them to their load and carried on.

The cold was intense. Fine snow found its way through the fur-lined hoods and melted on sweaty necks. Teeth ached as the frigid air was drawn into burning lungs. Muscles screamed and shivered uncontrollably, causing both dogs and men to fall time and time again, but they carried on, and, as Fitzgerald recorded in his diary, "Nooned one hour above Colin's cabin...." After travelling for another twenty-five kilometres, they came across an abandoned First Nations camp, prompting Fitzgerald to call it quits for the day. It was 3:25 p.m. Under normal circumstances, the men would have been jubilant, but today they had no energy for joy.

The dogs were fed and bedded down. Exhaustion and strain showed in their tired eyes. Heads hung low; energy had been spent. Before long their breathing slowed and all settled to sleep. Each man in the patrol tended efficiently to his duty. Once the meal was ready, they plowed into their plates. This food was nothing like what was being served back in Fort McPherson — no caribou steak, vegetables, starchy buns, or First Nations delicacies, just the standard beans, bacon, and bannock, but Fitzgerald and the men made the best of what they had, and were undoubtedly grateful to be under a roof.

Fitzgerald made the daily entry into his logbook. Since they had left Fort McPherson they had travelled 105 kilometres.[3] This distance was good, considering that the weather was becoming increasingly worse as the days progressed. But they were in the Arctic — wind, temperatures, and snow were beyond their control. What they had to do was to follow the map of the Dawson-Fort McPherson trail that had been drawn for them by Special Constable Hubert Darrell,[4] keep on the correct course, and fulfill their orders. They called it an early night, resting bone-tired bodies.

Cabins in the Yukon were often built on stilts, or raised platforms, to accommodate the accumulations of snow and also for protection from the wildlife.

A letter hangs on a tripod for pick-up by a passing winter patrol. Delivering the mail was another duty of the RNWMP.

30 BELOW. SUNDAY, DEC. 25TH. LIGHT N.W. WIND WITH HEAVY MIST.

In what seemed a blink of an eye, the rising-time alarm went off. It was Christmas Day. But for this patrol it was not a day to have a holiday or slow the pace. Instead of celebrating with family or friends, the Mounties were breaking a trail by 8:00 a.m. Nostalgic memories would have to suffice. Today, they would look for the cache of extra dog food that had been placed along the trail prior to their departure. To help lighten initial loads on the sleds, it was common practice to have carefully hidden provisions placed along the trail for patrols. Since the amount of dry fish to feed the dog teams for thirty days weighed hundreds of kilograms, a cache had been made about one hundred kilometres out from Fort McPherson.

The air was thick with moisture again and visibility reduced as they rejoined the trail alongside the Peel River. The going, Fitzgerald noted, "was heavy." They persevered, searching their way through a landscape that, except for the ghostly silhouettes of trees lining the river, was a featureless expanse of white nothingness. At 10:45 a.m, they found the mouth of Trail Creek. It was there that they found the cache of dried fish. It took the men an hour to rearrange the loads to include the fish, but before noon they were once again making headway, continuing to mush up along the banks of Trail Creek. Soon they found a "fresh trail," and their travel became somewhat easier.

At 2:15 p.m. they stopped for the day, thirteen kilometres upstream from the mouth of Trail Creek. According to Fitzgerald's diary, they had covered another twenty-six kilometres, a remarkable distance considering they had had to stop and repack the sleds. At this point it appears that Fitzgerald assumed they had completed the first leg of their journey successfully, since there is no suggestion in his diary to the contrary. What he and his men did not realize was that they had missed a turnoff, and, by taking the "fresh trail," they had made a mistake. In fact, they were not on the planned route. The fresh trail they had found was not the regular route taken between Fort McPherson and Dawson City. Hindsight, however, suggests that it would have been easy to make a mistake when navigating in limited light through winter terrain cloaked in dense fog.

The trail they mistakenly followed led to what they saw as another stroke of luck — another old Native encampment. They utilized what was at hand and were prepared for the night when darkness edged out the dim twilight. There was no moon visible, no stars to lighten the sky, just the orange flames from the fire to give warmth and a sense of comfort and calm on this Christmas night. The men sat around the fire, smoking their pipes, with steaming mugs cupped in their hands. They could hear the water of Trail Creek running under the icy surface nearby, and if they looked, all along the water's edge there was the crusting of ice that looked almost luminous in the firelight. It was a very peaceful, still evening, so still that one could almost hear the snowflakes landing.

All were most likely lost in their own thoughts of Christmases past, and memories of family traditions. The isolated life of a Mountie in the North is one that few men would seek out. Sleep was sometimes a very welcome distraction from days filled with cold, hunger, and hard work and often very little else to bring them cheer. On this Christmas night, at least, they had one another for company.

24 BELOW. MONDAY, DEC. 26TH. STRONG S.E. WIND, WITH HEAVY MIST.

The men were up and getting ready in what was known as the "dead hour" before dawn — the time when brains didn't quite function with the rest of the body. By 7:30 a.m. they were back on the trail, but they knew within a few short hours that the combination of the snowy landscape and darkness would be making grey ghosts of the trees lining the creek.

The dogs had recovered from their ordeal of the previous day. Ever since they found the "fresh trail" following the creek, the early going was good. But this was about to change. After only a few hours of peering through the heavy mist, headaches throbbed behind the men's straining eyes. A raw headwind bit at their faces and they had to keep facial skin covered in the protective warmth of their fur-trimmed hoods. Only thirty seconds of exposure to this extreme cold could cause frostbite.

At 1:45 p.m., they had a second stroke of luck when they came across an encampment of local Natives, and they quickly befriended the group. So far, it had been a good day. They had travelled another thirty kilometres and covered this distance in only six hours, one hour of which had been a lunch stop. Fitzgerald's diary for the 26th stated that the going was very good. But the inspector's satisfaction could not have lasted long. He soon found out from their new friends that they were now just over thirty kilometres "up" Trail Creek. Somehow they had missed their route turn-off the day before.

This unfortunate fact was brought to Fitzgerald's attention by one of the Native men, Esau George, after he looked at the RNWMP map. In George's opinion, this map was poorly done, but since he knew from experience the route the patrol should have been on, he knew they were off location. Carter was supposed to have known the route, but he had failed to recognize the needed turnoff. The unsettling news prompted Fitzgerald to immediately hire Esau George to guide them back on the trail leading to Dawson City. Carter's mistake was understandable since he had only been on the patrol in the reverse direction. Still, this failure could have been disastrous had they not stumbled across the encampment of First Nations people.

The patrol set up camp within the cluster of Native tents and were grateful for the many hands that helped them. They walked out the dogs, and then chained them to trees, as usual. On this night it was easy to make beds for them out of branches from the plentiful black spruce trees. Low-hanging branches were chopped and laid out for each one. Now off the snow, the dogs didn't need to use as much energy to keep warm, thus saving on food consumption and the use of reserves. Once the dogs were fed and watered, cold noses once again touched tails and they were bedded down and quiet on the heavily scented boughs. Occasionally a "yip" or growl was heard as muscles relaxed and sleep came.

It was a clear night made special by the sharing of food and good company. The black sky was salted with stars. The northern lights began their dance, starting with shades of blue, fireweed pink, iridescent greens, flashing into flame, and dying out high in the atmosphere, only to begin again. It has been said that on a still night a buzzing sound can be heard from the lights, and, if the sky is especially clear, black stars[5] can be seen. The men swapped stories around the campfire and enjoyed the sense of camaraderie. A moon rose into the darkened sky and cast their shadows on the snow. Those familiar with the North know that being there can bring a profound sense of peace.

Aching muscles began to loosen, and finally it was time to call it a day. Fitzgerald finished recording his daily log, and the four headed into their tent. The fire continued to burn with flames shooting into the still air, almost reflecting the movement of the blue-green lights above them. The northern lights continued to shimmer in the black velvety sky, but with a warning for the morrow. This beauty would bring with it plunging temperatures.

FOUR
Esau George Guides the Patrol

This is the law of the Yukon,
and ever she makes it plain:
Send not your foolish and feeble;
Send me your strong and your sane —[1]

Fitzgerald offered the First Nations guide Esau George a payment of $3 per day to lead them back to the correct trail, which he accepted. He would get the patrol back to the route the men were meant to be following, a section of the trail known as the Big Portage. Once this was accomplished, the Aboriginal guide would be paid and he would return to his family.

Rather than retrace the patrol's route into the Native encampment, George led them another eight kilometres up Trail Creek and then headed due south on a very small creek for eleven kilometres. The going was excruciatingly difficult and Fitzgerald noted in his diary, "Going very bad all day, had to break through three feet of snow and only made about 12 miles." Hearts raced, muscles burned, and their breath became gasps. Eyelids froze shut and lips turned blue in the extreme cold.

At 2:00 p.m. the exhausted group stopped. They had covered a mere twenty kilometres, but the patrol could not carry on. Not only had they been beaten by a savage southeasterly wind, they had climbed over 250 metres up the side of an unnamed mountain with each step sinking into a metre-depth of loose snow. The climb was nearly vertical, with nothing to hold onto and almost nothing to focus on in the white landscape. In a move that had slowed them down even further, the Mounties had strapped on their regular snowshoes, which were small in comparison to the snowshoes normally used by the Natives for a long journey into the wilderness. Their snowshoes sank deep into the snow with each step, making it very difficult to gain firm footing. George's snowshoes, on the other hand, were a good thirty centimetres longer and wider, giving the guide more stability on the snow.[2]

The dogs were completely worn out. The men unharnessed them and chained them to trees, but some refused to eat and drink. Barely able to move, they just wanted to sleep. Even in their state of extreme exhaustion, Constable Kinney and Esau George were sent ahead to make the trail for the following day. Fitzgerald wanted to be sure that all was prepared as much as possible for the next leg of the journey. He hoped snow would not begin to fall that night and wipe out the trail the two men were preparing.

The remaining men gathered wood for a fire and quickly had dinner underway. They brewed a pot of tea, and by the time Kinney and George returned to camp, their meal was ready. Again, the men ate in relative silence as they tried to consume the food before the bitter cold froze it on their plates. Boiling tea was added to tin cups every few minutes to melt the quickly-freezing liquid. Gradually, with warm food settling in their stomachs, a hot drink giving them warmth, and a fire piled high with wood, they could settle into some relaxing conversation.

Since the patrol was at a higher elevation than the previous night, the mists that had accompanied them had now dissipated, and their camp was surrounded by high peaks. As the stars gleamed overhead, Fitzgerald shared the story of how the Mounties, with the help of the Aboriginal people, protected the Arctic boundaries for Canada. The North was a place that many countries wanted to claim as their own, and countries such as Norway and the United States were challenging Canada's sovereignty.

This story, one that Fitzgerald knew well, was about the "Mountie and the Muskox," and his friend and fellow officer, Major J.D. Moody, who had been very involved. All the men were aware that being a mounted police officer in the frontier meant that policies and procedures could be made as the need arose. The NWMP were considered "government" in remote areas,[3] and the story of the Mountie and the Muskox was one such piece of history, and one in which Major J.D. (John Douglas) Moody took the initiative that confirmed the ownership of the North by the Dominion Government of Canada.

The little audience settled on their log seats as Fitzgerald continued:

———◆———

In 1880, Great Britain transferred possession of the Arctic islands to Canada, but the government in Ottawa paid little attention to the possession of this frozen "wasteland." That is, until a Norwegian surveyor began to take an interest in the same area. By 1902, Otto Sverdrup had made extensive surveys and scientific studies in the North, and had mapped many of the islands. Sverdrup built a small rock cairn and planted a Norwegian flag on top and proclaimed possession of all the islands he surveyed for Norway. He tucked this proclamation into a cognac bottle, leaving it atop the cairn.

While the Norwegian government ignored Sverdrup's activities, they served as a wakeup call to the Dominion government. John A. Macdonald decided that a manned detachment would be the most effective way to oversee any further exploration and possible claims of the Canadian North by other countries. The detachment would be built from the ground up, and so all materials for its construction, from lumber to windows to bedding, were shipped North aboard the 421-metric tonne wooden sailing vessel, the *Neptune*.[4]

The *Neptune* set sail in the spring of 1903, with J.D. Moody aboard. The ship stopped in at the whaling stations in Cumberland Sound and continued into the Hudson Bay. Even before his arrival on Herschel Island, Moody got to work. When in Fullerton Harbour (in present-day Nunavut), he observed the increasing trade in muskox skins. A man sensitive to the needs of the indigenous people, he was concerned and curious about those who were responsible for this. Moody decided to investigate.

No doubt, Esau knew that the muskox has a long history in the North. It is believed that some 90,000 years ago, before human footsteps on the North American continent, a strange, shaggy-looking, hairy creature crossed the dry land of the Bering Straits from Siberia to the far North. They settled in a region called Glacial Refugia, in the northern Arctic islands.[5] These strange animals, completely covered by a nearly black coat, the hair of which can measure up to sixty centimetres long, have small furry ears, a short tail, and rounded hooves with very sharp edges. They have exceptional hearing, eyesight, and sense of smell. Large, sweeping, curved horns, which darken as the animal ages, can grow to twenty centimetres in length.

The Native people called them *oomingmaks*, the bearded ones. The Europeans called them muskoxen. These ancient animals spent eight months of each year in the frozen North, and four out of those months in almost complete darkness with temperatures of -30 to -40°C, without the windchill.[6] Although they were primarily a food source, all parts of the animal had value — the skin was used for bedding and clothing, and their horns were carved into utensils and tools. Now, it seemed, someone was slaughtering vast numbers of these creatures and shipping their hides to Europe.

Moody immediately issued a proclamation forbidding the killing of muskoxen for trade purposes. The animals could continue to be hunted for food, but not for trading, since their numbers were declining at an alarming rate. If this rampant trade was not addressed immediately, the food source for the First Nations could be seriously diminished, and the herds may be even annihilated.

Moody's declaration left no doubt that the Canadian government, through the NWMP presence, would continue to actively enforce regulations and restrictions on their land in the North.[7] The Arctic islands with manned detachments flying the British flag would serve as a reminder that the boundaries of Canada included the Arctic islands, since they had been transferred to the young nation just two decades before. Moody's stance also established a conservation practice while confirming the ownership of the Arctic lands, a practice that continues to this day.

———————•———————

Seven years later, this story reminded the group how the NWMP worked to protect the Native peoples and their livelihood in the North. Their pipe smoke blended with the fragrance of spruce wood that was being consumed by the flames, and, in the stillness, one could almost smell the temperature dropping. Darkness enveloped the small group, and soon the only sound was the crackling of the fire. It was time to rest. The next day would be another difficult one, for the group would be continuing their ascent of Caribou Born Mountain.

43 BELOW. WEDNESDAY, DEC. 28TH. FINE, VERY COLD.

By 8:00 a.m. the group was on the move. Once more, Kinney and George had been sent ahead, travelling up a ravine. The trail made the late afternoon before by the two men was now barely passable, and the little party struggled up a very steep incline of three hundred metres. According to Fitzgerald's diary, "Climbed 1000 feet from camp until 1 p.m. At the head of the mountain the climb from Trail Creek is 1800 feet." Once again, they were climbing a nearly vertical wall of ice and snow. The dogs were becoming increasingly exhausted as their backs humped, straining into their traces, landing with each jump in a metre of snow, only to do the same jump again and again, while pulling the sleds loaded with gear.

Glenbow Archives, PD-383-2-19.

When the terrain became to difficult for the dogs to pull their loads, the winter patrol would often double up the dog teams, haul the toboggans with supplies up the slope, and then return for the next load.

The weary men and dogs stopped for lunch and were munching their food when Esau George's Aboriginal group caught up with them. They all took a break together. They had reached the upper end of Caribou Born Mountain.

At this point, Fitzgerald made the decision to stop for the day, and at 2:30 p.m. just minutes after the sun had set, they made up camp. The distance covered that day had been only twenty kilometres, but it seemed like twice that.

Frostbite was a concern, so while some daylight remained, each man checked the face of another. Although the down-filled parka hoods were fur-lined, the wind easily found a way to nip at noses, lips, and cheeks. With temperatures reaching such bitter lows, the body's natural defense against hypothermia (a condition when the body's core temperature drops to 28°C can lead to cardiac arrhythmia and possible death) will constrict blood vessels closest to the skin. This helps to protect vital organs, but with reduced circulation, patches of exposed skin can easily become frostbitten. This means that it becomes itchy or painful, with white, red, or yellow patches on the skin's surface. If the affected area becomes numb, attention is needed to quickly thaw it somehow. More severe degrees of frostbite involve hard blisters that quickly turn black or purple with time. Once the skin starts to peel or fall off, the person is in real danger of gangrene, which can be fatal. Luckily for the patrol, there were no signs of frostbite or hypothermia.

With that concern averted, the men made camp, looking after the exhausted dogs, setting up the tents, and building a fire. By this time, the practice had taken on the quality of a well-oiled machine. The First Nations families had caught up with the patrol, and there would be a sharing of food and company again. With the gathering darkness edging out twilight, the wind seemed to hush and that quiet stillness returned. Nature, now peaceful, showed a different side of her character from the raw cruelty of the day.

They had been climbing steadily since Trail Creek and it seemed as if they were on top of the world. It would be another clear night, and once again the sky filled with fiery lights, woven high up in the atmosphere, mirroring the flames of their fire. Fitzgerald described in his diary the troublesome mists they had encountered on the north slope of Caribou Born Mountain.

Caribou Born Mountain is a mountain in the Richardson Range, and unbeknownst to the men, some two hundred million years ago the area in which they camped was once an ancient tropical sea. Coral reefs and the creatures that swam among them[8] are preserved as fossils in the area limestone and other sedimentary rocks that are up to ten kilometres thick. But this once-surging life was now buried under an accumulation of snow, and the past lay in silence. The next leg of their trek would take them down through the Richardson Range and into the low-lying river area of Dawson City, the raucous gold-rush town of 1896.

More branches and deadfall were thrown onto the fire, and they all sat down to eat. The frozen stillness gradually soothed them and they were finally able to relax after what had been an extremely taxing day. It was good to be with those who knew the area well and who were generous in sharing extra food and giving assistance where needed. Even decades after the March West, their unique relationship with the First Nations was still much in evidence.

The Gwich'in tribe, or People of the Caribou, have been a part of this area for millennia, and are the most northern of all the First Nations. Their legends and stories have been passed down from generation to generation, and the legend of their arrival to this land has deep spiritual roots.

———————◆———————

The Sky Spirit looked down upon the empty earth. Deciding there needed to be someone to take care of it, the Sky Spirit sent Raven down to observe the land of the frozen North. As Raven flew over the region, he decided to create Wolf, or Amaruq. Amaruq's spirit would be a teacher, offering guidance and teamwork; it was a powerful animal of guardianship and community. Wolf would roam the lands and carry a message of discipline and order.[9] The Sky Spirit was pleased, but wanted more. Raven decided then to create Man and gave man a larger spirit than Wolf. Both Man and Wolf would live in harmony, with one dependent on the other.

Raven also created Caribou, and the Gwich'in people took their name from the herd animals that were always on the move. This creature provided food, skins for clothing, shelter, and blankets, and the bones and antlers were made into weapons and utensils. Sinew was spun into threads. Nothing of the Caribou was ever wasted. Importantly as well, man had a spiritual belief that in every Caribou, there was a piece of Man's heart, and in every human's heart there is a piece of Caribou. The Gwich'in believed they could think like the caribou.

Man killed the strongest caribou for his needs, but then the caribou numbers started to decline, as the weak were not able to sustain a growing herd. Man asked Wolf for help, and he asked Wolf to keep the caribou strong by killing the weakest in the herds. So for centuries, Wolf helped Man to keep the caribou herd strong.

———◆———

There may have been wolf eyes watching the smoke of the fire, or there even could have been caribou silently looking on. No one knew, but one thing all did know as they sat at the fire that evening was how humans who inhabited this harsh and remote place depended for their lives on the animals in whose midst they dwelt.

Embers were glowing red hot in the fire pits and it was time to add more fuel to keep the flames alive while they slept. Spruce needles caught fire in a crackling flare. The setting was peaceful, unbelievably so, but beyond this small group silhouetted against the flames, were forces of nature across the vast expanse of the territory, all of which had the potential to be fierce, even cruel. This thought, however, was likely far from their minds as they slipped into tents and drifted off to sleep.

FIVE
A New Year

I am the land that listens,
I am the land that broods;
Steeped in eternal beauty,
crystalline waters and woods.[1]

34 BELOW. THURSDAY, DEC. 29. FINE. CLEAR AND COLD, THE VALLEY VERY MISTY IN HILLS.
It was another bitter morning. Cold crept up from the frozen ground and
seeped in through the thin walls of the tent, prompting an early rise. The
dying embers from the night before sprang to life again when poked by
long sticks and fed with additional brittle deadwood. A pot of coffee boiled,
and bacon was soon sizzling in the frying pans. Breakfast would not be a
leisurely meal, but one hastily gulped down so the patrol could be on the
move by 8:00 a.m.

The group descended Caribou Born Mountain for half a kilometre,
slipping and falling as they went. Their rest had done nothing to dissipate
the muscle aches from the previous day and now strained thighs added to
the pain. With Esau George in the lead, they were on the lookout for a
small creek, planning to follow it until it emptied into the Caribou River.

A very slight whisper of running water was barely audible under the
sound of the panting dogs, hoarse voices, and the grating of the toboggans

on the rough icy path. More snow had accumulated, making travel slow, but they doggedly kept going on to the limit of endurance for both men and dogs. It took great amounts of exertion to push and pull the sleds when they got stuck in a drift. The men broke out into a sweat, increasing their risk of dehydration. Unless they continued to drink, hypothermia would not be far behind. Waves of exhaustion engulfed them. In all likelihood, if Esau George had not been guiding the patrol, they would have been lost forever in this wild place.

The sharp peaks of the mountains gradually threw off the mists of morning and loomed against the cold, grey sky. The men did not stop for lunch and instead continued the long heart-breaking struggle along the creek. Finally they arrived at Caribou River, the start of the next portage. It was time to call it quits for the day. But the day was not over as the dogs needed tending and their camp was to be set up.

Now nine days into their thirty-day patrol, the dogs were showing signs of fatigue and would have to be watched carefully. After devouring their dried fish, the worn-out pack settled on their spruce branch beds and fell into a deep slumber. It would be a while yet before the men could do the same.

The world around them was quiet with the stillness having returned in the gathering dusk —a relief after the energy-draining day. Challenges of the North can reduce any man to despair, yet it can also bring a very real sense of peace. Frayed nerves began to calm as the men dealt with their nightly tasks. Shouldering the axe, one of the men went to chop green wood for the fire, hoping to find dead wood as well. Billows of smoke brought tears to the men's eyes and added flavour to their supper. The homely smell of frying bannock filled the air, and the pot of beans bubbled in the cast iron, its earthy flavour enlivened with the addition of a can of corned beef. Coffee was sweetened with canned milk and sugar, and a dessert of dried fruit filled out the menu.

After dinner Fitzgerald finished his report, noting the dogs were very tired and that they had travelled twenty-three more kilometres. During the day they had not encountered any hoped-for wild game to supplement their food stock, but perhaps the following days would be more fruitful.

Sitting around the campfire was their time to talk. One by one the men tamped tobacco into pipes with cold-roughened fingers. It was Constable Richard O'Hara Taylor's turn to tell his story. He also had an interesting past. Prior to joining the Mounties, he had worked for the White Star Cruise Line, a luxury cruise company that began sailing from Liverpool to Australia in 1842, and later to Canada and the United States. Taylor was a seasoned traveller, trained in navigation, and used to the regimented life of an officer. While crossing the rough Atlantic Ocean to Canada, he had opportunities to learn about the Mounties, and decided to enlist in the growing force.

Taylor's dinner, served on a tin plate in the remote frozen wilderness, was nothing like the gourmet food served on fine linen, china, and silver service used by the bejewelled diners in the ship's mahogany-panelled dining rooms, but the idea of becoming a Mountie had captured him.[2] He used his disciplined training to face the challenges of policing in the young land. Had he remained with the White Star Line, he most probably would have been a part of the growing excitement surrounding the construction of largest ship in the fleet, the "unsinkable" *Titanic*. For Taylor, constellation gazing on clear nights took on a different meaning than it did for most since he had learned to navigate by the stars while working on the ship.

Behind the men, the sky had darkened and filled with the stars that Taylor knew so well. It would be another spectacular show of the Aurora Borealis, its brilliant colours shimmering as before. He added snow to the coffee pot, which was hanging by a cross-pole supported by two forked stakes. Coffee and smoking helped to pass the evening as they stretched their cramped legs. The lights flaring above were a welcome distraction from their cares. It always took some time to adjust to the conditions of travel on the trail, and the conditions they faced had been fierce. Winter patrols always tested the body — that was to be expected — but also the mind. It was finally time to turn in and sleep.

51 BELOW. FRIDAY, DEC. 30. FINE WITH LIGHT S. WIND.

Day ten and they were on the trail by 8:15 a. m. Snow had filled the portage and with each step the disturbed powder billowed up and found a new place to land. The dogs were buried with every jump. Pulling as a team in such an environment was almost impossible. The officers continued to assist hauling the sleds. They had to clamber up steep hills and their progress was halted, time and again. Because the going was so slow, the risk of hypothermia was never far off. It was the worst possible footing. Sweat from their continued effort froze and their clothes clung to their bodies like icy armour. Temperatures of -45°C with a slight headwind can feel more like -60°C. They suffered acutely from the bitter cold and surely must have felt a sense of desperation. At 2:30 p.m., Fitzgerald stopped the patrol, even though they had not completed the portage. It was essential for them to warm up.

The five men set up camp in record time, and once they had changed into dry clothing, the sweat-soaked ones were hung beside the fire to dry. Steam rose from the damp clothes as the heat of the flames drew out the moisture. Luckily, the night was clear and there was no sign of snow. Their clothing would be dry by morning.

Preparing the evening meal became habitual. Even though it was only mid-afternoon they had not stopped for lunch, so this meal would be a big one, and they deserved it. The day had taken its toll on both men and dogs,

Glenbow Archives, NA-513-9.

Breaking trail on what was known as the Big Portage. The portage, a term used here to describe a "short cut" that allowed the patrol to avoid an extended meander of the Peel River, was an astonishing 130 kilometres long.

and they urgently needed food high in fat and fibre to rebuild strength. The dogs may have also been given an extra fish to help build up their endurance for the next segment of the journey. The fourteen kilometres they had covered that day must have been a disappointing distance. If they didn't pick up the pace, the patrol would take longer than their target of thirty days, and, if they went over their expected time, they would need to find animals to shoot for food. So far they had seen nothing, but Esau George knew there were ptarmigan in the vicinity. Snaring the plump northern bird or two would give them a very tasty meal and a welcome change from bacon, beans, and bannock.

Fitzgerald and George once again looked at the map the Mounties had been given to follow when they left Fort McPherson. The Native guide would take them to the mouth of Mountain Creek. From Mountain Creek, George estimated the time to reach Dawson City would be about fifteen days — that was if they had good travelling conditions. With luck they should reach their destination by January 15, quicker than their original thirty-day patrol estimate. This was a very uplifting bit of news.

Sitting around the campfire and staring towards the heavens hastened their drowsiness. They piled more wood on the fire, crawled into the tent, and bundled up inside their sleeping blankets. Sleep was their only escape from the cold.

40 BELOW. SATURDAY, DEC. 31ST. FINE WITH STRONG S. WIND. SAW THE SUN TODAY.

It was New Year's Eve. It seemed they had barely slept before they were forced out into the frigid day again. With a ferocious wind rattling the thin walls of the tent, it seemed pointless to try to get back to sleep. This would be a very cold day on the trail. Strong winds would drop temperatures to almost -70°C and those winds would whip up blowing snow.

They were barely back on the trail when their eyes began to sting, the force of the wind sucking moisture out of them. Particles of ice crystals hitting any exposed area of the skin made it feel like an attack of thousands of biting insects. The terrain varied little from the previous day and the gruelling efforts had to be sustained. Every sense was in overdrive as they crept, ever so slowly, towards their destination at Dawson City.

Cold-stiffened fingers held onto leather harnesses, trying to give any assistance possible to the struggling dogs, and even to tipping the toboggan on one edge, balancing it so it could "skate" and achieve greater speed with less resistance.

The one hour of sunlight, appearing above the horizon at 1:28 p.m. on December 31, seemed to mock them. Largely blocked by the high mountains, it shone down on an angle, casting strange shadows that moved with the blowing white flakes. Above them, riding on the high altitude winds, were soft wispy clouds but there was nothing soft or gentle about their location. They trudged on — a test of both strength and endurance. At 3:00 p.m. they stopped.

The intense cold must have numbed all thought and tasks were done robotically — tending the dogs, building a fire, changing out of sweat-soaked clothing, setting up the tent, unloading the gear from the toboggans, and checking the runners and finally checking snowshoes for signs of deterioration. Did they feel like eating once food was ready?

On this, the last night of the year, there was little energy available for a celebration. But with George's guidance they had avoided the disaster of being lost in the Yukon, and this reason alone was cause to celebrate.

The winter patrol took eight days to cross the Big Portage. Being out in the open, without the protection of the timber belt, meant that they would be exposed to sudden shifts in weather conditions.

Although they would not be dancing or enjoying time with family and friends, they could rest easily knowing that they were now going in the right direction. With luck on their side, in less than twenty days they would be in Dawson.

———◆———

Dawson was the "little" city that had a population of 16,000, which had grown to a total mining population of 30,000 during the 1896 Gold Rush, with an estimated 100,000 gold seekers having passed through the boisterous community. By 1898 it was the largest city west of Winnipeg and north of Seattle. The raucous legendary party town was only four hundred kilometres away from where the patrol sat in silence around the fire.

There were stories that the ghosts of Yukon stampeders who had lost their lives on the Chilkoot and White Pass Trails came back to haunt the saloons and bawdy houses in perpetual drunken merrymaking, as if it were New Year's every night. However, there was no illicit behavior on any Sunday, as the NWMP had ensured these establishments were closed on that day of the week.

Hundreds of gold seekers line the Dawson City docks, waiting for the first boat heading down the Yukon River, circa 1898.

Initially, First Nations, miners, and traders inhabited the Yukon, but with the discovery of gold in Rabbit Creek, promptly renamed Bonanza Creek, the situation changed dramatically. In a sudden flurry of activity, tens of thousands of frenzied stampeders made their way to the North in search of "easy gold." Once again Canada's northern boundaries were being threatened, and so were the lifestyles of the Aboriginal people. Nineteen officers of the NWMP were sent to manage the situation, but that proved to be not enough.

Within two years, the Yukon force swelled to 285 members, with Superintendent Samuel Benfield Steele arriving to assess the activity. Banks and gold shipments had to be guarded, law and order kept, alcohol trading with the First Nations had to be stopped, and the North West Mounted Police and the Union Jack flag became symbols of security for those who ventured into the Yukon after struggling over the summits that provided access to the area.

A tent city sprang up at the base of the Chilkoot Pass, where the NWMP were stationed with their weigh scales. Prospectors were able to purchase the required supplies at the base of the Pass for exorbitant amounts. Candles were $5 per box and potatoes were 50 cents a pound.

At an elevation of just under 1,000 metres, the Chilkoot summit was a frightening place. The trail to the top is fifty-three kilometres long, yet the rise for the last one kilometre is 305 metres — truly a vertical struggle. The stampeders called the Chilkoot Trail the "golden staircase." Gold seekers hauled their cumbersome packs up the steep and treacherous path, climbing the 1,500 steps carved out of snow and ice. Since pack animals could not travel this route, often the prospectors would stash part of their gear, go back down the mountain, pick up more, and repeat the process, or they would pay someone to help carry the loads. It was an agonizing ordeal.

There was another route into the Canadian gold fields that was even worse, if that was possible. The White Pass, known as "Dead Horse Trail," was used by some of the 100,000 stampeders. At an elevation of 875 metres, with a death-defying drop on one side, the trail was so narrow, slippery, and steep that 3,000 pack animals met their demise by falling into the canyon below, most likely hitting jagged ice-covered rocks on the way down. One portion of the trail was called Dead Horse Gulch, in memory of all the hard-working horses that met their end in a pile at the bottom of the canyon. When a pack animal went over, so did the miners' supplies.[3]

Tents, supplies, and sled dogs multiplied as the numbers of prospectors grew. Here, a RNWMP officer oversees the packing of supplies, ensuring that it represents the required "one ton" of goods. The Chilkoot Summit lies between Alaska and British Columbia.

Trail conditions weren't the only obstacle; there were the extreme temperature fluctuations as well. In the winter, the mercury dropped to -55°C while in the summer it could rise over a hundred degrees to 50°C.[4] The other very real concern was the availability of sufficient supplies to last through the winter. The NWMP built a weigh station at the base of the Chilkoot Pass. There, every traveller crossing the border into Canada would meet the NWMP officers and have their goods weighed. The police had established a mandatory supply list for all those who ventured along the routes. The predetermined list meant that packs had to be heavy. Each stampeder was required to weigh his supplies and was not permitted to on the trail unless he had a .9 metric tonne of food and provisions — the amount needed for one year of prospecting in the gold fields.

The list was lengthy and included such items as heavy-knit sweaters, flannel shirts, overalls, blankets, a waterproof blanket, twelve bandanas, one stiff-brim cowboy hat, hip rubber boots, a waterproof coat, heavy socks,

Glenbow Archives, PD-383-1-54.

Three prospectors headed for the gold fields take their lives in hand as they run the rapids between Lindeman and Bennett Lakes, British Columbia. In 1898, the NWMP counted 850 boats under construction at Bennett Lake.

long underwear, and mitts. Food items included forty-five kilograms of navy beans, sixty kilograms of bacon, and 181 kilograms of flour, as well as a quantity of rolled oats, corn meal, and rice, along with a sufficient sugar, coffee, tea, dried potatoes, dried fruit, and laundry soap. The list was extensive, designed to ensure the well being of the prospector for one year. Just because the eager stampeder made it to the weigh station with required supplies, didn't mean he had reached his final destination. He still had to travel across Bennett Lake and then eight hundred kilometres down the raging waters of the Yukon River to Dawson City.

Prospectors had to build their own boats, but during the winter all water travel was halted because of freeze-up. During these months, the NWMP were actively building latrines to minimize the spread of diseases, in addition to keeping law and order during the time everyone waited. When the ice did break up on Bennett Lake, the race was on again. Boats broke apart in the wild rapids, claiming countless men and their supply of goods. There was nothing straightforward about laying a claim for gold in the Yukon. The territory was not going to surrender her riches easily. It was, however, estimated that during 1893, $300,000 worth of gold was discovered in the Yukon. Today, that would be in excess of $27 million.[5]

The NWMP, with members of Canada's militia known as the Yukon Field Force assisting for protection, took bags of money from Bennett Lake to Victoria, British Columbia.

In protecting the growth of the young nation, this time specifically in the North, the NWMP once again received government recognition for their efforts. Sent there because of the tumultuous conditions of the Gold Rush, they skillfully managed the throngs of people who flocked to the Yukon and established the continued presence of the law along the Dominions northern borders. Their presence in the North was even more necessary since Canadian boundaries were being questioned more frequently after the discovery of the mineral wealth in the region.

Just shortly after the Gold Rush ended, Inspector Fitzgerald, a sergeant at the time, and four others were sent to Fort McPherson, with orders to explore the area. There was a need for detachments in the western Arctic. The international focus on the North and the opening up of Canada's Arctic frontier, meant that the visible presence of NWMP was essential.

———◆———

The scene, just a few years prior in the same general area, was so very different from the New Year's night of 1910. The men who sat around the campfire with their nearby teams of sleeping dogs could not have been in a seemingly more different place, although the experiences and training gained during those Gold Rush years certainly had an impact on their ongoing type of policing.

Did they wait to bring in the New Year or talk about their plans to head home after they finished the posting in the Arctic? Maybe they spoke of a postponed celebratory meal when they arrived in Dawson City, but, if so, Fitzgerald never wrote a word about it in the last entry of his log for 1910.

SIX

The Peel River Canyon

Staggering blind through the storm-whirl,
stumbling mad through the snow,
Frozen stiff in the ice-pack,
brittle and bent like a bow;[1]

37 BELOW. SUNDAY, JAN. 1, 1911. HEAVY SNOWSTORM ALL DAY.

If this New Year's Day was a sign of things to come, the patrol was in trouble. The men had a late start at 8:45 a.m, and headed into a raging blizzard to once more do battle with the elements. Storms in the Yukon wilderness are not child's play. Visibility had been reduced to nothing, hampering the men's ability to negotiate the formidable rumpled drifts of snow that grew in the wind and played havoc with the toboggans. Loads were spilled when the sled's runner caught and rode up the side of an unseen steep bank and had to be righted. Travelling alongside the tree-lined creek presented another hazard since the toboggans bumped into trees, causing carefully balanced branches to dump their accumulation of snow on the heads of the already burdened patrol below. It was a brutal morning as they made their way toward Dawson, carving a route where established trails had disappeared under layers of falling snow.

The tempo of the storm increased as the day continued. Wind-driven snow chafed their skin along the edges of their parkas. Energy drained out of them as they tugged and pushed their way alongside the toboggans. The one metre of snow that had fallen meant that the dogs were no longer able to pull without assistance. Struggling to drag themselves through waist-high snow and pull the dogs along with them, the men could barely move. But then, six kilometres up from the mouth of Mountain Creek, they came upon a small cabin — a welcome stroke of luck. Fitzgerald decided to stop for the day and spend the night in the log abode, even though it was only 2:00 p.m. and they had covered just eighteen kilometres, slightly over half of their target of thirty. Having a roof over their heads and protection from the storm was not only sensible but was life saving.

It was a terrible storm and the dogs had to be protected from the elements as much as possible. In weather like this the sleds were often used as a barrier to protect them. After stowing the gear in the cabin, the men dug a trench and lay the toboggans on their sides, creating a low fence to act as a windbreak. The huskies still had to be chained to trees, but there was no shortage of trunks for this purpose along the riverbank and within a short time all had eaten and were sheltering from the wind.

Once inside the cabin, the men unpacked their gear and set up for a night of relative comfort. The aroma of cooking pushed the frosty air out of

Log cabins nestled in the black spruce were always a welcome relief for winter patrols.

the cabin as the New Year's Day meal was being prepared. Fitzgerald wrote in his log that the going had been "very heavy" and that he had paid Esau George for five days of travel plus the three-day trip back to his family, for a total of $24. From here on, Fitzgerald assumed, they would be fine without their guide. He reasoned they were on the correct trail and they would have no further problems getting through to Dawson City with their mailbag and dispatches. Since both Carter and Fitzgerald had done this patrol in the reverse direction, all were confident that they could manage on their own. What Fitzgerald seemingly did not keep in mind, however, was the fact that the terrain can look very different when heading in the opposite direction. Carter's skills as a guide would soon be put to the test — and found wanting. Fitzgerald had made the fatal mistake.

During their long afternoon and evening they heard the wind increase in velocity, moaning as it hit the wooden walls and bent its way around the corners of the cabin. The eerie foreboding sound was almost like the voice of Death calling out. Every now and then the snow blew in through openings in the log walls as it had done on their first night out of Fort McPherson. Before long the spruce branches had dried out and the men placed their sleeping rolls on top of them. After the day's demanding struggle, it was good to lie down and stretch stiff, aching legs. Sometimes just staring at the ceiling was all that was needed for them to relax. Snores soon filled the cabin, only stopping when muscle spasms from painfully contorted feet, legs, and hands woke the sleeper. The cramps were so powerful that often a strong push was needed to restore limbs to straightness.

Outside, fresh snow was slowly burying the dogs. But this was a good thing. Falling snowflakes trap a high percentage of air as they land, thus creating a form of insulation. Because the air can't easily move, it heats up and creates a cozy space almost like an igloo. The warm sleeping dogs were snug and comfortable even though a powerful blizzard was intensifying just centimetres above them.

35 BELOW. MONDAY, JAN. 2ND. HEAVY SNOW STORM DURING THE NIGHT AND ALL DAY.

By 7:30 a.m. stomachs were filled with warm food and coffee, all gear had been packed up, toboggans loaded, and the dogs hitched to the line. The men were on their own without their First Nations guide. It would turn out to be a day when they could have used the strength of one more man.

The ferocious snowstorm continued, and, if that wasn't enough to create sufficient difficulties, the men had to hack their way through the bush. The activity was made more complicated because the dogs had to be kept still while on the line so they would not end up in a tangle, with snapping teeth and flying fur as the men focused on cutting a trail. Frozen brush can be cut through quickly, but sharp branches and trunks can snap back, whipping faces and eyes. Cutting, dragging, piling, moving the dogs and sleds forward just metres at a time, only to repeat the process again and again was torture. But there was no alternative. Even though the edges of the river they were following were frozen, "driftwood" debris piled high along the banks prevented the men from using nature's trail of ice.

The collection of branches and trees that had accumulated on the Peel River occured during the river's cycle of freezing and thawing. Once spring break-up begins, the rushing waters and chunks of ice grab anything in their way and pull it along until stopped by an outcrop of rock or some other natural blockage. The pile grows and becomes a nuisance to any person or animal needing to make a crossing. It was this debris that was thwarting the efforts of the patrol. They were forced to carry on cutting a trail as they went, which added more distance and time to their journey, all while being punished by the unrelenting snowstorm and a savage wind.

At noon they stopped to eat and to rest, but it wasn't really a rest. Out came the camp stove, the cooking gear, ingredients for lunch, bowls for the dogs' water, which had to be melted from snow — the list seemed endless. The hour sped past and before they knew it they were back at it again, hacking down brush and making their way along the riverbank with its pile of broken trees and logs.

By 2:15 p.m. what little light they had was failing, so they stopped and set up camp by the edge of the river, eight kilometres above Mountain Creek. They had covered another sixteen kilometres that day, which was good considering the difficulties they faced. In the overall picture, however, the distance wasn't what they had hoped to achieve; this would mean more days on the trail to Dawson City. But it was the end of their thirteenth day on the trail and time to get warm by the fire.

Sitting in front of a fire with flames licking the black night sky helped the patrol to unwind and regroup. They ate their evening meal and listened to the sounds of the running water under the ice from the nearby river. The Peel River area, with its six tributaries, is home to such Arctic animals as the wolverine, grizzly bear, pine marten, and peregrine falcon, as well as the wolf and caribou, and is the ancient cultural landscape for First Nations. For those who know how to find wildlife, the area is teeming with food.

The Hart, Snake, Wind, Bonnet Plume, and Blackstone Rivers all find their way to empty into the mighty Peel, which passes Fort McPherson and then flows into the MacKenzie River, which empties into the Arctic Ocean. In the winter months, the Peel region is spectacularly rugged, covered with snow and ice. Its pristine beauty and solitude can nourish the soul, and that was exactly what Fitzgerald and the men needed that night to renew their spiritual strength.

After another meal of boiled beans and bannock, it was time to tend to their nightly camp chores. Fitzgerald finished writing his log, documenting the distance the patrol had covered, and observing that the going was very heavy due to the deep snow. Kinney and Taylor cleaned up the dishes and chopped more wood for the fire, and Carter checked the toboggans and snowshoes for signs of wear and made any repairs he could. He did this as he sat by the light cast by the flames all the while absorbing the heat of the fire. Sitting close to the fire was a sharp contrast to the air just a few metres away and Carter was glad to be near the warmth. His face, nearly frozen during their travels, was now burning as it slowly thawed.

Once all the tasks were complete it was time for the men to sit and have their nightly conversation over scalding mugs of tea and their pipes. Flicking a match with his thumbnail, Fitzgerald watched the sulfur head flare instantly. It made him recall the winter of 1908 at Herschel Island, the world's most Northerly police post. Fitzgerald commented, "When there are no ships wintering at Herschel Island, I think that it is one of the most lonesome places on earth. There is no place one can go...."[2]

During that particular winter, the Canadian government, jointly with the American Museum of Natural History, sent an expedition to the Arctic to study the Inuit. Vilhjalmur Stefansson, a very well-known Arctic explorer, was leading the group. He had some supplies but had forgotten to include matches. Thinking this might cause a problem, Stefansson bought 1,000 wooden matches from a captain of a whaling ship, but the smokers in his group thought this amount was hardly enough to sustain them throughout the winter, so they refused to begin the journey without more. Since there were supply ships due to arrive at Herschel Island, the group decided to wait.

Days passed and the ships did not arrive in the harbour, causing Stefansson to approach Fitzgerald and made the request to purchase more matches. Fitzgerald inquired about the amount of food and provisions the expedition was taking, and, when he discovered they were not taking any food for the journey, he staunchly refused to supply matches, since he believed that the expedition would end in disaster. From his experience, expecting to totally live off the land would likely culminate with starvation of the entire group, and then the necessity of sending out a rescue party.[3]

Fitzgerald, or "Northern Man,"[4] as he was known, was well aware of the potential danger in assuming food could be obtained along any northern trek during the winter months. The refusal to supply the expedition matches caused international attention with Fitzgerald being in the

Glenbow Archives, PA-3886-27-4.

In the 1890s to early 1900s, hundreds of American men would winter at Herschel Island, waiting for the ice of the Arctic Ocean to thaw and release their ships. During this time, buildings were raised, theatrical performances were given, and even sports leagues were formed — anything to help pass the long wait.

headlines as confronting the well-known explorer and suggesting he was ill-equipped and not adequately prepared for the assignment he had been given. Fitzgerald offered a cabin and supplies to the group to winter at Herschel Island, but insisted that if the team planned to go with sufficient food supplies, he would not give them any matches.

Fitzgerald's remarks and actions had the desired effect, and, although Vilhjalmur Stefansson and the expedition did not stay on Herschel Island, he took Fitzgerald's advice and bought enough food and matches for the journey from another whaling ship. Ironically, Fitzgerald did not take his own advice. Two years later, he was leading his patrol with the expectation of at least supplementing their food stores with wild game along the routes. Having neglected to pack appropriate hunting gear, Fitzgerald had put himself in the same vulnerable position as Stefansson would have found himself had he decided to proceed without adequate supplies.

The police detachment at that time, consisting of two sod houses and a storehouse for winter supplies, had been set up to monitor the American whalers and the trading of alcohol with the Inuit people. Fitzgerald made it clear to the whalers that any trade in alcohol must cease and duties would be collected on whales killed in Canadian waters. In addition to those duties, he was also in charge of monitoring and ensuring the safety of people who passed within the vicinity of the tiny isolated post. The members of the winter patrol were well aware that Fitzgerald paid scrupulous attention to detail.

———◆———

The evening was almost at an end. Another day on the trail was complete and they could only hope that tomorrow would be an easier one. Their quiet evenings of camaraderie offered relief after the struggles they faced and obstacles they had to overcome each day. Still, sometimes it must have felt as if the long winter nights weren't long enough to help them regain their vigour.

Once they had added more chopped spruce to the flames, the four headed into their tent, after shaking the flaps and brushing the accumulation of snow off their parkas. They lit candles to help them find their spots, then settled in for some well-deserved sleep. From the outside, the tent was just a candle-lit canvas square illuminated against the enormous tranquil river valley. One by one the flickering lights were extinguished and the light was swallowed by the darkness.

46 BELOW. TUESDAY, JAN. 3RD. LIGHT SNOW ALL DAY.

The men were up and busy while morning was still dark. One tended to the meal while the others headed outside to dig the toboggans out of the snow that had been blown onto the windbreak. By morning the barrier was almost hidden in the new snowfall. Once the dogs heard their masters coming, a few popped their sleepy heads out of the white winter blanket, but there wasn't the usual chaotic greeting. Today was different. The dogs were fatigued and appeared to have some reservations about getting out of their warm snowy burrows. The trek was taking its toll.

So far the patrol had covered 312 kilometres in the thirteen days out, and the going had been anything but easy. They had broken trail almost the entire way, crossed the portage, climbed a mountain, and descended down a slick precipitous mountainside. The dogs had met headwinds, tugged and pulled through fresh snow, sinking well past their shoulders with each leap. They were worn out. No yips or barks filled the air on this frosty morning, and some even rejected the dried fish. This was not a good sign.

The snow was still lightly falling, but the day looked more manageable and maybe day fourteen would bring them luck. By 7:30 a.m. the patrol had eaten, packed up their camp, harnessed the reluctant dogs, and were running beside the huskies to help them get on the move. Today the men would be heading through the Peel River Canyon to the mouth of the Wind River.

The canyon walls rise straight up from the banks the Peel River, between sixty and 150 metres in height. Formed of folded sedimentary rock, these dramatic walls stand as if on guard, protecting against any intruders who attempt entry into this desolate, ominous place. Snow clung to the vertical rocks, but not quite enough to soften the sharpness of the crags. There was beauty within the towering walls, but this was not the time to admire surroundings. They kept on going.

At lunch they took a break, ate, had something warm to drink, and then were on the move again. They had hoped that as they mushed along they would find some wildlife taking refuge in the canyon. Perhaps they would find an animal to shoot, which would add much needed variety and nutrition to their meals. They had no such luck, however, and would have to be content with another night of beans, bacon, bannock, and maybe some dried fruit.

Although they kept a lookout for tracks, they resumed their trail-breaking as a light snow continued to fall. One kilometre above the lower end of the Peel Canyon, they found the mouth of the Wind River and turned to follow it.

The Wind River was magical. The fast-moving river itself is an aquamarine colour, which is reflected in the ice when frozen. The hue added to the supernatural effect. Buried under the ice lay multi-coloured gravel, worn smooth by constant motion. The patrol, familiar with the beauty of this area during the summer months, once again had no time to admire their surroundings on this wintry day.

By 3:30 p.m., when the dogs refused to pull any further and the dim winter light was failing, the men came across a trapper's tent. They knew the trapper, and like most trappers of the day, he had left his trapline for the winter and headed away to perhaps Dawson or even further south. His tent would give them another night's break from the work of setting up their own, but that didn't mean they still didn't have to contend with the drudgery of the dogs, the gear, the camp stove, the cutting of spruce boughs, the checking on snowshoes and sleds, and the building of a fire.

They set about their individual tasks, looking forward to settling in for the evening in the shelter of the tent. Fitzgerald updated his log, noting, "[the] going very heavy; dogs about played out." They had covered another nineteen kilometres, again less than their anticipated daily distance of thirty kilometres. They would have to pick up the pace or they would be out of food before reaching Dawson, unless they met another First Nations group and could buy some, or they managed to shoot some game. This reality was disquieting.

SEVEN
The Wrath of Nature

The winter! The brightness that blinds you,
The white land locked tight as a drum,
The cold fear that follows and finds you,
The silence that bludgeons you dumb.[1]

47 BELOW. WEDNESDAY, JAN. 4TH. STRONG S.E. WIND WITH SNOW.

Rolling out of warm sleeping blankets to face temperatures of such raw extremes must have been automatic; others would have balked at what lay ahead, but duty called. Match heads flared in the darkness as the men held the flames to light the frozen wicks of their candles. Finally, after much sputtering and popping, enough wax was melted for the thawed string to catch fire and cast a light inside the canvas walls. The comforting glow was in absolute contrast to the outside environment, but the patrol wasted no time in beginning their day.

Stomachs growled and throats were parched, a result of the strenuous exertion of the previous days. During sleep, even in subzero temperatures, a person can lose one litre of water through sweat. The combination of dehydration from the physically draining work of the past two weeks and the nightly water loss caused their throats to feel like they were coated with razor blades. No matter how much liquid they drank it never seemed enough.

After a pot of snow had been melted, they gulped down as much liquid as they could hold, quickly devoured their morning bannock, then tackled their morning duties so they could start making a trail.

The men continued to mush along the contours of the Wind River and would follow the river until they reached another mountain pass, which would take them over Mount Deception. The mountain with an elevation of about eight hundred metres was their next tough obstacle to cross. After going through the pass, they would look for the mouth of Forrest Creek. Esau George had estimated they should be in Dawson by January 15, only eleven days away. Getting there would be a very welcome relief for the patrol. They were being battered each and every day, and the weather showed no signs of changing.

Conditions on the morning of January 4 were atrocious. The vicious headwind was an unseen force that made every step an ordeal. They could not pause to rest for fear of being blown backwards. Each man leaned into the wind with his head turned to avoid a full-face blast, but this hardly made a difference. The frigid air made breathing almost impossible; every laboured gasp the men took was filled with frozen icy particles that entered and melted in their lungs. Bouts of coughing wracked their already sore bodies. The dogs were also coughing as they ran, a cause for concern since fluid in a dog's lung could quickly develop into a very serious problem.

The snow continued to blanket the land and the tamped-down path made by the trailblazer first thing in the morning was completely obliterated within an hour. It had been a total waste of time. The dogs had no firm footing and sank with each leap forward. The smaller dogs were buried every time they tried to pull their load. The men took charge of the sleds, giving the most possible assistance to the tiring huskies. Surely it would get better. They didn't think about it for too long. Thinking about it would not change anything.

At noon they stopped for a break. The storm, however, did not let up and continued to unleash its wrath, but the men did manage to find refuge in the shelter of a tree and they began preparing some food. The dogs were so tired, they just collapsed into heaps in the deep snow. Many sought out warmth from their teammates and fell into a deep slumber, but not for long. The hour had passed quickly and they were once again heading into the quickening tempo of the blizzard. In these blinding conditions it would be easy to miss an important turn off.

The calls of "Mush!" and "Gee!," meaning "head right," and "Haw!," meaning "head left," were muffled in the forceful blasts.[2] The men might as well have had a very firm hand clamped over their mouths, as the commands were muted by the force of the wind. The wind speed increased, slamming against the branches and trunks of the trees, setting up ear-shattering vibrations. Trees that lined the riverbed provided the natural instruments for the aerial symphony, yet there was nothing musical about the shrill sounds that were being made. The dogs had their ears pinned back in an attempt to block out the sound and protect their sensitive ears. The unceasing din was overpowering and physically draining, yet there was no getting away from it.

They continued as long as they could muster the stamina to do so. The officers and the dogs worked as a cohesive unit and the power of the relationship was not taken for granted. The men relied on the dogs and, while on the patrol, their lives depended on the health of the dog teams, just as the animals looked to the Mounties for care. Each day they struggled together in the wilds of the Yukon the bond of trust and loyalty grew.

At 2:30 p.m., after an excruciating six hours, they stopped. All hands tended to the weary teams. When the temperature drops to such extremes and snow falls, the ground surface takes on the quality of sandpaper and the dogs' large rounded paws showed signs of abrasion. The men carefully inspected eyes for brightness and checked their gums to make sure they were pink and moist. The underside of each dog was also examined for frostbite, since this vulnerable hairless part of their bodies can be susceptible to freezing. They also watched anxiously to see whether the dogs were eating. A poor appetite was one of the signs of declining health.

Next, the Mounties made a snowbank to serve as a windbreak and cut black spruce branches for the dogs' beds. As the temperature continued to drop, the huskies huddled together signalling they wanted to have shared warmth. Huddling would help them to reserve what energy they had left. A dog's ability to tolerate extreme cold weather depended on age, nutritional status, health, and coat density, and at this point in the patrol they were tiring and turning to each other for comfort. It was important they maintain the ability to stay warm, if not, their health would deteriorate rapidly.

Huskies are bred to withstand sub zero temperatures. Below the longer outer wiry fur, the soft undercoat acts as an insulator and helps the animal to adapt to the frigid conditions. If snow begins to melt on the dog's outer fur, then the men would know that they were dealing with a sick dog. A healthy dog can be covered in snow, but an ailing dog, or one who is becoming intolerant of the cold, will have ice on their fur, showing they are losing enough body heat to melt the fresh flakes. Allowing those dogs who wanted to sleep in a heap to do so was the kindest thing the men could do for their hard-working friends. Although they were pack animals, the dogs were often considered as family by the officers who patrolled in the very remote regions of the Dominion.

Once the dogs were curled up and content, the men then set to work getting themselves ready for another brutally cold night. Taylor carried a barometer in his pocket, and, upon reading it, noticed it showed that the pressure was on the rise — an indicator that lower temperatures were on the way, as if -43°C wasn't already cold enough. The fire began to edge out the cold and at least when around the blaze the men absorbed some heat. The orange and yellow flames, barely visible through the dense smoke, cast a glow on the snow, and the world took on a more peaceful state.

While Fitzgerald recorded in his log that they had covered another sixteen kilometres, Taylor, Kinney, and Carter tended to other mundane chores of camp. Soon the food was ready, the tent set up, and sweat-soaked clothes were once more hanging by the heat of the fire. Every now and then a spark shot out of the blaze and singed a pair of pants or wet socks, sending a small plume of smoke into the air. Its acrid odour blended with the blue tobacco-scented spirals from pipes and steam from mugs of tea, not to mention the rank woollies of the men.

As they relaxed over their hot drinks, Fitzgerald recalled another patrol in his career, one in which he almost lost his life.

———◆———

It was while posted at the detachment on Herschel Island's rocky out-crop and he was with Constable F.D. Sutherland. They were monitoring the increase in the number of the American whaling ships that used the

Canadian harbour as a place to winter. As each ship came into the harbour, Fitzgerald and Sutherland, wearing their official uniforms, met the captains and informed them of the laws that must be obeyed and the duties that they would be collecting on the whales taken from the Dominion's waters.

The Pacific Steam Whaling Company from the United States had six ships intent on wintering at Herschel Island, so they would be ready to harvest the whales once the thaw occurred. In 1890, a whale had an estimated worth of $10,000, a staggering amount for the time, and during a seventeen year span from 1889–1906, over 1,300 whales were slaughtered.[3] The Canadian government wanted the duties owed and it was the job of the NWMP to collect them from the foreign companies. Fitzgerald made this clear to the captains. The captains were also informed that no alcohol trading with the First Nations would be tolerated. A few weeks later, once Fitzgerald was confident the laws were being obeyed, he left with Sutherland to attend to needs at Fort McPherson, leaving a Constable Thompson alone and in charge.

The two men boarded their wooden boat, laden with supplies, and headed out on their 480-kilometre journey across the Arctic Ocean on their way to Fort McPherson. Weather in the far North can change rapidly; winds suddenly began whipping up waves on the surface. For two days Fitzgerald and Sutherland's small boat was tossed about in the chilly froth. The storm smashed the boat to pieces, ripping planks off the sides and creating a harrowing ordeal for the men. Thankfully, they were able to reach a sandbar before the boat was completely destroyed, and thus were able to scramble to safety and set up a very basic camp. The provisions they had packed with them, if not sunk to the bottom of the ocean, were ruined by the salt water. They were left with some rabbit meat for food and falling snow for water. Numb with cold and without any means of communication, they waited stoically for the remote possibility of a passing boat. Fortunately, they were spotted by a passing Inuit whaleboat and crew who picked them up and took them on to Fort McPherson. It was luck indeed that saved the two from a cruel death on a shrinking sandbar in the Arctic Ocean.[4]

The early patrols Fitzgerald completed between Herschel Island and Fort McPherson and Dawson City were never done without the element of danger. In reality, the northern patrols, whether overland or by sea, were dangerous, no matter what time of year. The possibility of death by exposure to the elements was a constant companion.

———————◆———————

Fitzgerald could see that it was going to be another cold night, and so more wood was piled onto the fire. The fire would also help warm the air the dogs were breathing and in turn keep them as comfortable as possible. They lay in quiet slumber and an occasional yip or whimper escaped from the pile of snowflake-dusted fur. By this point in their trek they had lost any animosity among themselves and were content to be in a pile of noses and tails. Taking inspiration from the peaceful dogs, the men decided to call an end to their day.

Rising up from their seats of chopped wood, the four stretched their stiffened legs, rinsed their cups in dishwater, shook the snow from their parkas, and crawled into the tent. The spruce boughs under their sleeping rolls were soft and aromatic, and the men were asleep almost immediately. Outside the wind whispered, announcing the rapid decrease of temperature, dropping to a dangerous low.

65 BELOW. THURSDAY, JAN. 5TH. FINE WITH SLIGHT HEAD WIND.

The clear sky brought with it heart-stopping temperatures. It was really too cold to even attempt leaving the comfort and safety of their tent, yet following orders, off they went. It would be another day of testing endurance and will power. At these temperatures skin freezes almost instantly. Moisture from the men's breath froze in icy shards on their faces only to be melted when exhaling and refrozen upon inhaling. Their lungs screamed in agony, the result of laboured breathing and a tightening and burning sensation in their chests.

After four hours of this torture, Fitzgerald wrote: "only went about six miles [10 kilometres] when we had to go in the bush and make camp at noon owing to the intense cold, some slight frostbites among the party." They set up camp, and got a fire going.

After fifteen days on the trail, heading in a southerly direction, the patrol had hoped the going would be getting easier, but that was certainly not the case. Their challenges seemed to grow with each passing day. As the daylight paled, a clear black sky appeared above them, and before long the northern lights danced. It was, however, just too cold to enjoy any of the brilliant splendour and the men headed into the tent to try and to get warm and thaw out, and deal with the pain and prickling on the frostbitten areas. Frostbite can become a medical emergency, and, if not treated properly, could become serious. Rubbing their hands together to create heat, the men could then cover the worst frostbitten areas with their hands and gradually bring circulation back to the hard and waxy-looking frozen skin.

Light from the candles filled the tent and the men took some comfort inside the flimsy walls as they gradually warmed up. With each passing day the bond among the men continued to grow. They knew each other's hopes for the future and experiences of the past. They understood each other in ways most never would. The training they all received gave them the knowledge and appreciation for what it was they had taken an oath to do, and the courage, commitment, and dedication required to fulfill their duty. But all that aside, these were men who were being battered by nature each day and needed sleep to regain sufficient strength to survive the next day and the next.

EIGHT
Arctic Deep Freeze

Honor the High North ever and ever,
Whether she crown you, or whether she slay;
Suffer her fury, cherish and love her—
He who would rule he must learn to obey.[1]

54 BELOW. FRIDAY, JAN. 6TH. VERY STRONG HEAD WIND IN PM WITH HEAVY MIST.

It was day seventeen and the patrol awoke to brutal temperatures. There was a harshness in the life-giving air, almost as if the men were being dared to even try and breathe. A temperature of -48°C, plus a wind chill caused by the headwinds, would set the temperature somewhere near -85°C. It was an exercise in sheer will power to face the day. They may well have felt that their purpose on this patrol had been frozen along with the world that surrounded them. Was it worth this effort to deliver the dispatches and custom duties collected?

The day was a blur. Fitzgerald wrote: "Left camp at 8:30 a.m. Could not noon on account of open water as we could not get on shore." His diary entry isn't clear as to the actual difficulty faced with the "open water," but he noted that the open water of the Wind River had caused problems while they were trying to reach the route over Mount Deception. It is possible that the high winds blew driftwood and branches, breaking up the iced-over surface of the river, covering the shore with debris, and making it impossible to find a suitable place to stop. Patches of water showed black against the white snow-covered rocks that lined the river-bed, giving the landscape a stark oppressive look. Blundering through the thick scrub, frozen and brittle, took every molecule of energy they had. Wave after wave of tiredness overcame them until it must have seemed that there was simply nothing left inside.

As Fitzgerald indicated, there was no stopping that day for lunch. They continued on their way, facing the punishing wind with every step they took. Finally, the hostile wind began to die, and with that a pale cloud-like glimmer appeared, and a mist suddenly enveloped them. They could not go on. Fitzgerald continued: "Camped — 3 p.m. at the lower end of Mount Deception. Going very heavy and lots of trouble with open water. 11 Miles [18 kilometres]."

Setting up camp in the thick, pervasive fog was eerie, with the heavy mist clinging to the stunted trees and shrouding them as they worked. They could hear the sounds of one another moving about and the panting dogs, yet could not see them. Chopping down trees to get a fire going, unloading the sleds, setting up the tent — the tasks were done almost blindly, were but done in due course. Within a remarkably quick time, the patrol sat down to eat.

The food was nourishing and comforting. Then out came pipes and more coffee. Sitting around the smoky campfire in the cold mist, they stretched tired legs and shrugged aching shoulders that had been strained in their sockets for hours on end. The frostbites from the day added to their discomfort, and, in the heat of the fire, the thawing felt like thousands of needles piercing tender skin. Would they ever again feel dry and not achy or in pain? They should be in Dawson in nine more days, which was half the number of days they had been on the trail.

It would be another early rise. They cleaned up their utensils in the darkness, checked once more on the sleeping pack of dogs, piled more wood on the flames, shook the new snow off their jackets, and headed into the tent. Inside was damp and cold and just as inhospitable as it was outside. The candles, however, cast a glow and brightened up their space as they sorted through kits for maybe a drier pair of socks or undershirt.

There was no way to do laundry or properly dry things while on patrol, but keeping dry and warm was crucial to their well being. Since they had begun to feel the effects of frostbite from the temperatures brought on by the wind chill, they had to work hard to keep themselves in the best conditions possible.

They were tired and one by one they blew out their candles and bade each other goodnight. Sleep was the chance to dream of a different environment and take themselves away from the demanding orders given to them in this brutally harsh part of the world.

The noises of the Yukon continued as they had for millennia. As night wore on, the fire became a pile of embers that pulsed and popped, and occasionally a spark would shoot into the night air. A wolf would howl, the wind would whistle as it hit branches, and chunks of snow would drop to the ground with a soft thud. When the temperature hit that critical degree, the sap in a tree would freeze, splitting the truck open and sending the sound like a shotgun to shatter the tranquility.

The alarm clock shrilled inside the solitary little outpost of the tent, and all were jarred into consciousness with any dreams abruptly coming to an end. They began their daily habits with the usual grit. Dogs, cooking, packing up, trail blazing — each man had his job to do.

51 BELOW. SATURDAY, JAN. 7TH. FINE WITH SLIGHT FAIR WIND.

One day rolled into the next and again they were doing battle with the elements. At least on this day the trail that had been made early in the morning was not filled in by new snow by the time the dog teams were pulling. The wind, however, continued to chafe their frostbitten noses and cheeks. The pain must have been excruciating. Frozen fingertips and feet rendered movements wooden and halting, but this did not stop the patrol from helping the dogs to cover another twenty-one kilometres, putting them now less than ten kilometres below the Little Wind River. In the fading light of just before 3:00 in the afternoon, they set up their camp.

As they stirred beans into a pot of water, the men looked at their remaining food. Their supply was getting low and they still had at least another week on the trail, if not longer. They had seen no game tracks at all, but that was not surprising as the weather they were experiencing would turn out to be one of the coldest in recorded history in the area. Perhaps the wildlife had taken refuge in the shelter of trees or snow caves.

Nor had they seen another group of First Nations moving along the trail. To supplement their food stock, the patrols would often buy food for themselves or their dogs when they came into contact with the Aboriginal people. They would have to be vigilant and look for signs of any animals in the area. They had their .30-.30 rifle to hunt the large game, but needed to see something first. It was unfortunate that they had not packed any snares, since setting one at night might have produced a rabbit or some other smaller, yet nutritious source of food. For the time being they made do with what they had in the hopes that they would be in Dawson before they depleted the supplies they had. At least on this night the beans were hot and provided a much-needed meal.

They sat chewing their dried fruit for dessert, continually adding more boiling coffee to their tin mugs, which froze almost immediately. In fact, tossing boiling coffee into the air at temperatures so low will produce frozen vapour. The liquid will actually freeze in the air and form a suspended brown fog. The same applied to the dirty dishwater. The tossing of dishwater could have been a source of entertainment at the end of a very difficult and physically draining day.

The night was wearing on. In the clear sky the northern lights began to dance and the temperature dropped and dropped. Previously recorded temperatures were being broken as the men slept.

64 BELOW. SUNDAY, JAN 8TH. FINE WITH STRONG HEAD WIND.

The head wind made the temperature feel more like -98°C. Loose fine snow filled with frost particles were picked up and flung at the patrol, stinging faces and damaging eyes. Frostbites blistered, damaging another layer of sensitive skin. The men blundered on, senses dulled by exhaustion, but still demonstrating a remarkable stamina. By 1:30 p.m. they simply could not go on. They had covered a total of fourteen kilometres and were five kilometres up the Little Wind River, but the intense cold put an end to their day of patrolling. As before, this was by no means the end to their day.

The tasks started again. They staggered around the camp on shaking legs and hips. Frozen hands slipped off the axe handle and tips of ears throbbed in the cold. It seemed to take forever before they were watching the flames and huddling over their tea. The shadows fled the river valley and the men were once again in the darkness, while stars were single handedly trying to light up the sky. There were no sunsets where they were, just dim light fading to darkness. The scene must have matched their mental state.

The smell of the wood burning was calming and they soaked up the heat. Fitzgerald did a calculation and determined they had now covered over 410 kilometres since December 21, 1910, an average of twenty-two kilometres per day. They were two-thirds of the way to Dawson City. The difficult weather, however, made it seem unlikely they would reach Dawson by the 15th as Esau George had thought. But they hoped it would not be much later.

They tidied up their camp and crawled into the tent, shivering from a combination of cold and exhaustion. Consciousness began to slip away and snores bounced off the flimsy walls of their shelter.

22 BELOW. MONDAY, JAN. 9TH. FINE CLEAR DAY, SLIGHT SW WIND.

The day showed promise. Clear skies and warmer temperatures boosted their morale and they were off along the Little Wind River. The river squeezed its way out of the confines of the Illyd Range, and snow-covered mountains rose on either side of the narrow river channel. The beauty was remarkable, with ice crystals sparkling brilliantly in the slanting rays of the sun, even though it was only present for a very short time. What a change! The temperature had increased by over forty degrees, and, factoring in the wind chill, it had climbed over eighty degrees from the day before! It could not have been a more perfect day.

At lunchtime they called "Whoa!" and enjoyed a meal by the icy river. Kinney headed onto the ice and chopped a hole through the surface. When ice is thick enough, the pressure of cutting a hole causes the water to shoot like a geyser flooding the hole, making it easy to fill a pot with glacier water to be boiled for something hot to drink. Even the dogs seemed happier on this day and were loudly making pleas for scraps of the crunchy dough.

This day looked like a turning point. Nature had retracted her claws and surely things would be good going from now on.

By 1:00 p.m. they were heading out again and managed to cover a fair distance in a short time. With the increase in temperatures, though, by late afternoon the surface of the snow had become heavy and wet, and they stopped early. While the camp routine commenced, Fitzgerald calculated they covered another "16 miles [26 kilometres]," and that the "Going [was] very fair." More days like this and they would be making up time.

The men enjoyed a leisurely dinner and afterwards relaxed, puffing on their pipes. Fitzgerald had an interesting story about the area in which they camped. It actually had been the location of another very famous camp years a few years prior to their arrival there.

To maintain energy for the demanding physical exertion, the winter patrols had to stop, eat, hydrate, and rest. Here, the winter patrol takes a well-deserved lunch break on the Wind River portage.

———◆———

During the Klondike Gold Rush, a group of stampeders found themselves wintering in the region, waiting for safe passage into the gold fields. The weather was very unpleasant and typically gruelling, especially for those not equipped for the severity of the forces of nature. This group of just fewer than one hundred stampeders called their camp Wind City, most likely because of the forceful winds that blew between the mountains on either side of the river. The eager gold seekers couldn't wait to leave after spending the winter, but the name Wind River stuck.

Perhaps if Fitzgerald and the men were patrolling at a different time of year, the Mounties would have found interesting artifacts of those who wintered there in 1898. But now, whatever fascinating pieces of history remained were safely hidden for future travellers to stumble across, or for the Little Wind River to pick up and take downstream.[2]

———————◆———————

After a successful day the men, undoubtedly happy with their day on the trail, arranged their spruce boughs, wrapped themselves in their sleeping rolls and drifted off to sleep. As they slept, a fine layer of clouds moved in overhead, creating another blanket above the tiny camp and the temperature continued to rise.

13 BELOW. TUESDAY, JAN. 10TH. STRONG HEAD WIND WITH VERY FINE SNOW.

In what seemed a blink of an eye it was 8:00 in the morning and they were bundled up in their parkas and heading off. As the men travelled the bends and turns on the Little Wind River, the fine snow covering the frozen surface made it very slippery for the dogs. Traction was difficult and the sleds careened and bumped about. At least they were not battling with overflow when the wind broke up the ice, causing water to then gush and flow onto the trail. Fitzgerald wrote: "very little water to trouble us." This must have been a relief.

The conditions were worse than the day before, but they still managed to travel for six hours, all the while facing into a headwind. Their exposed skin must have continued to peel from the blistered frostbites by this point. They were also losing weight from a combination of the lack of proper food and overexertion.

A high calorie diet is required to help maintain and sustain the energy needed to keep the body warm in extreme cold temperatures, and when combined with intense physical work, even more nutrition is needed. The diet they were consuming each day was almost a starvation diet and they were becoming weaker with each kilometre they covered. Little did they know, it was about to get even worse. Without sufficient food, they would be unable to keep themselves warm, and, with a decrease of body temperature, would be susceptible to further health problems. However, on January 10 they thought all was going well enough for a successful trip into Dawson. They continued to watch for signs of wild game that had ventured out of shelters with the return of warmer temperatures.

As camp was being set up, they looked for tracks of wolf, or caribou, or other types of game nearby. It was becoming more apparent with each passing day that they would need to find food. Unfortunately, there was no sign of anything else living near them. It would be another dinner of beans and bacon and maybe even a can of tasty corned beef, laboriously opened with a small key that wound around the top. The razor-sharp edges of the can were a hazardous undertaking for frostbitten fingers.

Sitting in front of a roaring fire should have been a comfort, but instead the heat was agony to the frostbitten skin and chilled limbs. Heating up too quickly could easily burst small blood vessels close to the skin's surface, and so the men started with a gentle fire and then added the chopped wood as the night wore on. Another day had passed, and they were twenty-six kilometres closer to Dawson City. The distance covered had made it one of their better days.

The ancient majestic mountains, covered in thick snow and ice, cradled them on all sides. The narrow waterway of the Little Wind River ran under the ice, polishing the multi-colored stones, and the Milky Way streaked overhead. The constellations of the Great Bear and Orion flashed brilliantly in a velvety black sky. Then the lights began to dance.

Legends surround these spectacular lights. One story says that only spirits called *selamiut*, or Sky Dwellers, are permitted to pass into the heavens. Sky Dwellers have died either a self-sacrificed or violent death. To arrive in the heavens, one must tread over a very narrow and dangerous pathway through an abyss where the land and sea meet, and then through the opening of the great dome that is arched over the earth. The spirits who inhabit this place light torches to guide new spirits on the path, and these are the lights of the polar nights. Sometimes whistling and crackling sounds accompany the Aurora Borealis. These are the voices of the spirits trying to communicate with those on earth. Earthly beings must answer in a whisper.[3]

The men were sound asleep and did not whisper a response to the spirit voices that called them. Perhaps they were being told that they must carry on with caution. Or perhaps it was the voice of Death.

NINE

Forrest Creek Turnoff

Ye who know the Lone Trail
fain would follow it,
Through it lead to glory
or the darkness of the pit.[1]

22 BELOW. WEDNESDAY, JAN. 11TH. VERY MISTY WITH STRONG HEAD WIND.

Between the effects of an eerie mist and the winter morning darkness they had quite a time getting ready, but nonetheless they were at it again by 8:15 a.m. They were now in a timber belt where they hoped their luck would change and they would spot some large game. Maybe a moose or caribou would be sheltering in the woods. Either would certainly fill the dwindling food bag and give extra food for the tiring dogs too.

As the sleds gouged the trail the men were watchful for signs of wildlife, but the mist hung right to the ground, making it almost impossible to differentiate moist air from freshly fallen snow. Still, they remained vigilant for animal prints as they travelled along Little Wind River.

The fluctuations in temperatures and the strong winds had turned the river into overflow. Even with extreme cold temperatures, there was fresh water arising from springs. "Underground springs leaking out of the hillside find a way to the river and flow over the ice. If the ice cracks due to the weight of the dogsled and men, then the ice on the river can fracture, spewing pressurized frigid water from below over the surface wreaking havoc on traction."[2]

Piles of debris and water running over the frozen surface frustrated the Mounties as they mushed, with the sleds swaying from side to side. The dogs were pulling, slipping, falling, and struggling, desperate to gain some sort of firm footing. Frozen slush became embedded in their paws, but they continued, alert to the shouts of encouragement. The men's footwear was also taking on water, and their feet were wet and cold, but it didn't stop them. Not only were they contending with mist, wind, overflow, wet feet, and watching for any signs of wildlife, they were also on the lookout for the turnoff at Forrest Creek.

Forrest Creek empties into the Little Wind River. This small waterway would take the patrol across the Hart Divide and down the final run along the Little Hart River, to the Blackstone River, then on to Twelve Mile River (now called Chandindu River), to the Yukon River, and finally into Dawson City. They had just another two hundred or so kilometres to go, having already travelled nearly five hundred. If they could average about thirty kilometres for the next few days, they would be in Dawson in a week, by January 18 or 19. They had been on the trail for twenty-two days, and seven more would put them about right for a thirty-day patrol.

Whether they weren't paying attention or whether the mouth of the creek was so completely blocked by piles of broken trees and branches and overflow that they missed it will never be known. What is known is that they missed their turnoff and continued to do battle with overflow on the Little Wind River. Mushing past Forrest Creek would prove to be a fatal mistake.

At 3:30 p.m., and after "a very unpleasant day," according to Fitzgerald's diary, they built a fire and attempted to dry out their wet footwear and clothing. They had only covered fourteen kilometres that day. They had no idea they had missed their turnoff and were now heading in the wrong direction. The men carried on with the end-of-the-day jobs and were soon sitting at the fire, absorbing the warmth and eating their meal. The days were now routine: get up, break camp, mush, stop for lunch, mush, call "Whoa" before darkness completely descended, cut down trees, strip the branches for bedding, get poles for the tent and wood for the fire, then light a fire, unload the gear, set up the tent, with one officer chaining, checking and feeding the huskies, while another made their dinner. Then they ate, chatted around the fire, crawled into the tent and slept, all to be repeated, starting the next morning in the dark. And they were doing all this in temperatures and conditions that cannot even begin to be imagined.

The Mounties sat around the fire, and, as the black emptiness closed in, their eyes finally adjusted to the surroundings. The wind had changed and the mist steadily dissipated. They could see the beginnings of faint stars twinkle above. With the clear skies polar temperatures would slide down, but maybe that would help to freeze up the overflow, making the next day drier and easier for the dog teams.

On this evening, the camp took on a vestige of coziness. Quietness came with the night. Maybe it was the stillness; maybe it was the comforting smells of burning spruce, or the smell of snow-dampened leather harnesses drying by the fire. It could have been the warmth of their conversation, but whatever it was, there was peace. But that sense of tranquility would soon be shattered and replaced with a cold realization that would lead to desperation.

A moon rose over the rugged mountains, its pale beams making the snow and ice appear silver. Exhaustion overtook them. They cleaned up and headed into the tent. Consciousness slipped away and they were soon asleep.

37 BELOW. THURSDAY, JAN. 12TH. FINE; WITH SLIGHT HEAD WIND. A NICE DAY.

Ironically, Fitzgerald wrote that they awoke to a nice day and that the first three hours of were pleasant. There was no overflow. The trees, covered in snow, glistened in the sun's rays, giving them a Yuletide look. The iced-over river reflected a blue sky and appeared to match its aquamarine hue. Renewed in spirit, the patrol shouted encouragement to their teams. Tongues were hanging out of the huskies' mouths, causing the dogs to look as if they were smiling.

At noon they stopped for lunch. It was then they realized they had passed their turnoff to Forrest Creek and thus missed the route to take them over the divide. Fitzgerald acted immediately. He wrote in his log: "sent Carter to look for portage, but he could not find it. At 3:00 p.m. found that the river was getting very small." At that point they set up camp and once again Carter was sent out to find the mouth of Forrest Creek. For hours he searched until the twilight became darkness. He trudged back to camp with bad news. He did not recognize any aspect of the area and had not been able to find a creek that looked like the one they were to follow. Seemingly, they had travelled too far up the Little Wind River and would need to head back down the following morning. They had travelled nineteen kilometres but had no idea how far they had come beyond Forrest Creek.

This night took on a different tone. The fire's flames cast shadows, clouds moved in, and once more they were in the dark, but this time there was no sense of peace or tranquility but one of deep unease. Sleep would not come easily, if it came at all. Avoiding mistakes in the far reaches of the North does not guarantee survival, but a mistake almost always guarantees failure.

12 BELOW. FRIDAY, JAN 13TH. SNOWING WITH LIGHT FAIR WIND.

The patrol broke camp earlier than usual and were on the move by 7:30 a.m., travelling back down their trail from the day before and watching for the mouth of Forrest Creek. With only light snow falling, they made good time since their tracks were still visible and compact from the day before. After retracing their steps for kilometres down the Little Wind, they came across the mouth of a small creek. Relieved, they made the turnoff, and, thinking all was fine, settled down into assisting the dogs along the side of the creek bed.

Snow continued to fall, but, with the temperature warming from the day before, it was pleasant. All was going well until the creek became smaller and smaller until it became a trickle. There was no sign of a route over the divide. Realizing this was not Forrest Creek, they headed back down the six kilometres they had just covered. It wasn't yet noon. They had covered twenty kilometres and were still not on the right trail. When they arrived back at the Little Wind River, they headed down another three kilometres before setting up camp. It was only 1:30 p.m.

Fitzgerald decided they should get the nightly camp chores done and rest the dogs instead of further fruitless mushing. He wanted to find the Forrest Creek turnoff before dark and it was easier to do this by sending Carter out than driving all the teams up and down creeks to find the right one.

Carter headed further down the Little Wind. Each time he found a creek he would venture along the waterway looking for their route. He had been on the patrol four years prior, going in the opposite direction, but surely things wouldn't look all that different? He felt confident he could find Forrest Creek and was not about to admit defeat. Carter went up and down any and all streams, searching for anything that looked familiar. Finally, he found what he believed had to be Forrest Creek and headed back to camp with the news.

The patrol had spent two days looking, but now all seemed to be back on track, and the following morning they would head a few kilometres down the Little Wind and be heading on the correct trail. If the weather stayed on their side they should be able to make up the lost days and arrive in Dawson just before their food ran out. It would be touch and go, but if they arrived hungry, having not eaten for a day, that still would not be a problem. Their patrol would have been completed! Maybe this Friday the 13th wasn't bad luck after all!

Now that they thought they were just a few kilometres away from the turnoff, the evening passed in relative calm. The Mounties ate their beans, bacon and bannock, and drank hot tea. The sky cleared and the northern lights began. Shafts of crimson, blue and greens flung their shimmering splendour across the sky and over the snow-covered mountains. They buzzed and crackled. Once again, perhaps the "sky dwellers" were talking to the patrol.

23 BELOW. SATURDAY, JAN. 14TH. VERY STRONG GALE ALL DAY. COULD NOT LEAVE CAMP.

The wind blew with a force they had not experienced before on this patrol, assaulting their ears with threatening shrieks and wails. Inside the tent, the thin walls slammed in and out as though they were breathing. Trees broke in half, snapping with the sound of pistol shots. In these conditions, the men were risking their lives by going to check on and feed the dogs, which were huddled together with a snowbank for protection. The dogs were being buried as snowdrifts piled against them. At least they were keeping warm.

All the men could do was stay in the confines of the canvas walls. Their wet gear, hanging from a rope inside the tent, swayed with the blasts of the wind while the men waited for the storm to blow itself out. Maybe they sorted out their clothing to see what else they could wear to help keep them warm, or perhaps they mended snowshoes. Maybe they just ate and slept, catching up on some well-deserved rest. The good news was that Carter was certain that he had found the mouth of Forrest Creek, which would put them back on the right route, but the bad news was they had just lost another day. Their food supplies were dwindling and they were feeling the effects of poor nutrition.

39 BELOW. SUNDAY, JAN. 15TH. VERY MISTY WITH A SLIGHT HEAD WIND.

The alarm went off, rousing the men out of their slumber. The walls of the tent were quite still, indicating the gale had stopped. It was up and into action. They stuffed sleeping blankets into bags, dragged out the spruce boughs, took down the tent, fed the dogs and themselves, loaded the sleds, and were off once more by 7:30 a.m. Carter led them to the east branch of the Little Wind River and they would follow the contours of the waterway for twenty-six kilometres to the mouth of Forrest Creek.

The trail was cloaked in mist, requiring them to watch for hidden stumps, snowdrifts, and stones that could not only upset the sled, but also injure the dogs. Mist lay like smoke on the white snow and rippled when the dog teams ran through it. There was enough new snow on the trail to make the going a bit slower, and the runners of the sled gouged right down to the base of ice under the soft, wet surface. By afternoon, the trail was ice. The huskies were once again slipping and sliding but still pulled their loads. By mid-afternoon, as the sun was going down behind the mountains and casting long shadows across the snow, the dogs were tiring and slowing to a walk. Fitzgerald called a halt.

Like a well-oiled machine, and with swift and concise motions, the camp was soon set up and the evening meal served. Having eaten, Fitzgerald finished writing his diary saying: "[C]amped at 3:15 p.m. at what is supposed to be the mouth of Forrest Creek." This phrasing in his diary entry hinted that he was not convinced that Carter was correct in thinking they were at the mouth of the trail to take them over the divide to the Hart River, but they would learn the truth the following day.

The moon rose and lit up the ice on the river. All was tranquil again and the stillness was overpowering. They were alone in the darkness, isolated in the vast far reaches of the North. No one was there if they needed help; they only had each other for support. It was snowing, and every now and then the snow softly slid off the roof of the tent, joining the other night sounds. When exhaustion overtook them, they tapped the ashes out of their pipes and headed to their spruce-bough beds. It was the end of another day.

43 BELOW. MONDAY, JAN 16TH. FINE WITH VERY STRONG SW WIND.

By 7:45 a.m. they had packed their goods and were travelling up what Carter thought was Forrest Creek. Just under ten kilometres later they found the creek was dwindling in size. It must have been devastating for Carter and the rest. Their hopes dashed, they headed back to camp. While Kinney, Taylor, and Fitzgerald set up, Carter was again sent out to find Forrest Creek.

By this point the Mounties must have felt a sense of growing despair. Where were they? Why couldn't they find the creek? Both Fitzgerald and Carter had been on this patrol before, but neither was noticing anything familiar. That is not surprising, however, as they had both been on patrol in the opposite direction and those patrols had taken place several years before. But Carter had been confident he could guide the patrol, and Fitzgerald must have had faith in Carter, otherwise he could have paid Esau George to take them to Dawson. All other patrols had First Nations guides, so why did Fitzgerald feel they didn't need one?

They had not encountered any Aboriginal people since Esau George had been paid and left. Unless they met someone on the trail they would have only themselves to find their way. Carter searched and searched as the light faded. He came back to camp with bad news — "no success." Dismay must have given way to alarm for the patrol. They had covered

103 kilometres looking for the route over the divide in the past seven days, and on one of those days had been immobilized by the gale-force wind. Their food shortage was becoming critical, as was the supply for the dogs. The situation was grave.

TEN
"My Last Hope Is Gone"

23 Below. Tuesday Jan. 17th. Fine in a.m. with strong SW wind which turned to a gale in evening. Did not break camp. Sent Carter and Kinney off at 7:15 a.m. to follow a river going South by a little east, they returned at 3:30 p.m. and reported that it ran right up in the mountains and Carter said that it was not the right river. I left at 8 a.m. and followed a river running south but could not see any cuttings [trail markings] on it. Carter is completely lost and does not know one river from another. We have now only 10 lb of Flour and 8 lb of Bacon and some dried fish. My last hope is gone...."

— INSPECTOR FITZGERALD'S DIARY

As he was trained to do, Fitzgerald broke the problem down into the essentials and came to the devastating conclusion that must have been almost unbearable. They had failed. The men had travelled and searched for nine days along the Little Wind River for 157 kilometres, mostly through overflow.[1] The turnoff seemed to have simply vanished.

Fitzgerald wrote of his awareness of their dire situation and his recognition that there was no longer any possibility of success. Hope encourages the belief that there will be a positive outcome, but at this stage all hope was gone. How could this have happened? A patrol had never failed before.

An officer was fiercely committed to fulfilling orders, and that did not include failure. It simply was not an option. But he *had* failed. The implications of their dilemma raised horrific options — lacking food, they would need to kill and eat the dogs.

The suggestion of killing the dogs was one born of a desperate mind. Each dog that was killed would slow the patrol down and lengthen their travel time. The more days on the return trail, the more food they would need. Unless they shot some game, or met a group of First Nations or trappers, the dogs would be their only food source. They would serve a dual purpose, but one purpose would hinder the other. Turning around and going back to Fort McPherson on a diet of sled dog was tough to accept, yet he could see no other way.

Between December 21 and January 17 they had travelled 560 kilometres from the patrol start at Fort McPherson, and that didn't include the distances travelled without the dog teams, trudging on foot through the snow, just looking for Forrest Creek. Another 560 kilometres back, with just four-and-a-half kilograms of flour and three-and-a-half kilograms of bacon plus some dried fish for the dogs would not get them home. The situation was grim.

Taking everything in stride, because there was no choice, they made camp. The following day they would be homeward bound, backtracking on their trail to the Peel River. They needed some good luck. This was going to be a race of survival, a race against time, and a race against the forces of nature. Fitzgerald was determined that the patrol would win.

The men crawled into their tent after dinner. Did sleep come easily? In all likelihood it didn't. They were probably retracing their steps in their minds, recounting the twenty-eight days they had been on patrol and wondering how could all had gone so wrong. How could they have missed the blazed markers on the trees indicating the turnoff at Forrest Creek? Maybe there were none. Where were the moose? The caribou? The wolf? Where were the First Nations people? It seemed they were the only living souls in the area. But, most importantly, why had the inspector let Esau George go when he was willing to guide them to Dawson City? An excruciating possibility, and one that the men would never know, is that when Fitzgerald decided to turn back the patrol may have actually been on Forrest Creek, but had taken the wrong fork, which diminished to a trickle, leading them to believe they were on the wrong creek.

As the hours passed, a wind picked up and became gale force. It seemed as if their bad luck would stay with them.

13 BELOW. WEDNESDAY, JAN 18TH. LEFT CAMP, ON THE RETURN TO PEEL RIVER AT 7:45 A.M.

In the early morning darkness and the blasting wind, they picked up their trail and headed back the way they had come. The wind blew and their frost-bite blistered, peeling back the skin and exposing raw flesh. There was no point in shouting to the dogs, as the mushers' voices were just carried away, so they encouraged their canine partners by running beside them. It was more of a jog than a run. All legs were aching and tired and feeling the effects of malnourishment.

Retracing their journey just emphasized the vastness of the territory. The Yukon measured 482,443 square kilometres, and was covered with waterways and mountains. After eight gruelling hours, visibility was decreasing. They stopped to set up camp. The first thing they did was chop wood for a fire, but even the heat of the flames couldn't drive out the cold-ness from their nerves. Tonight they would kill one of the dogs for food. Fitzgerald recorded: "Killed the first dog tonight for dog feed, hardly any of the dogs would eat him, and had to give them a little dried fish."

Their pack of fifteen was now fourteen. Which dog had they chosen? Was it one who showed signs of illness? A sick dog can slow down a team. Was it one that was not a favourite? Was he a rebel? Nothing descriptive was written about it, but the act of raising the rifle, taking aim, and firing at one of their hard-working dogs is unimaginable. Crimson blood, the colour of the Royal Northwest Mounted Police wool tunics, splattered and flowed into the white snow. It was if the dog, in the act of dying, let it be known he had been a part of the RNWMP and his blood was his serge.

The worst was yet to come as the husky was then butchered and pieces of the dog given to his team to eat. This made the pack nervous. No wonder the dogs wouldn't eat their companion, and no wonder the men couldn't, either. The dog teams and the Mounties were a unit and there was mutual respect between the musher and his pack. This invisible unbreakable bond had been broken. They had just killed one of their own.

Fitzgerald continued in his diary that all the men ate that night was a small piece of bannock, made from the remaining flour, and a dried fish, which was the food brought for the dogs. They were reduced to a starvation diet, and with the physical exertion and the cold temperatures they would soon be very weak. The going would become almost impossible. Still, they had managed to cover thirty-two kilometres, which, despite their heart-breaking task, was one of their best distances on the trail.

The patrol understood each other without speaking words. They depended upon each other and the decision made by one would affect them all. This had been a terrible day, culminating in a meal that none were willing to eat. Sleep couldn't come soon enough. Perhaps they simply lay awake in a dazed half-world of consciousness, chilled to the bone, tired beyond belief, and with no hope.

28 BELOW. THURSDAY, JAN. 19TH. VERY MISTY WITH SLIGHT SW WIND.

By 7:30 a.m. the teams were harnessed, and the patrol was heading out on the trail. They could hardly find their way, for the mist lay heavily on the ground. Not only was mist an issue, the river was in overflow again, and for most of the day the patrol sloshed through ankle-deep water, glacier-chilled, trickling into boots and splashing up on their pants. Travelling through the overflow was unavoidable since cliffs came down sharply on both sides of the river. The curved front of the toboggan acted as a prow and the second and third sleds contended with the turbulence.

The dogs and men both suffered tremendously from paws and feet that were frozen and numb. Every now and then the river ice would crack, sending already anxious dogs into further unease. The patrol finally stopped for something hot to drink. Not only did they have to warm up but it was also necessary to check the paws of the dogs. Mushing in conditions like these can cause abrasions on the pads of their paws; undoubtedly, all were in agony.

They were back at it again for another few hours, slogging through the overflow and ghostly whiteness until they found a spot where they could make camp for the night. The men managed to collect some wood and lit a fire to dry their soggy footwear. Their feet were blue with the cold and they were miserable, but they had managed to cover another thirty-four kilometres — a Herculean effort. Fitzgerald wrote: "camped about 29 miles [forty-six kilometres] above the mouth of Little Wind River…." At the rate they were travelling, and, if conditions remained stable as they had for the past two days, they should make it back to Fort McPherson.

But food was a problem. Another dog was taken from the pack, and a shot rang out. The second one lay dead in a pool of scarlet. On this night the starving dogs did not refuse the meat. The patrol ate their meagre rations and drank tea, but did not eat dog meat. They just couldn't bring themselves to do so. The Mounties knew their own survival rested in food to fuel their bodies, but to eat the dog was something they were not yet able to do.

There was the faint beginning of stars, but nothing in the heavens could bring a sense of peace and quietness to their campfire. A desolate emptiness prevailed. The men were numb from cold and pins and needles pricked their thawing feet. The stabbing pain from frostbitten faces added to their discomfort, and then there were aching muscles, strained ligaments, and they hadn't felt warm in days. But most of all, they were burdened by a heavy sense of despair.

The North is unforgiving.

21 BELOW. FRIDAY, JAN. 20TH. VERY STRONG SW GALE ALL DAY.

Nature held the patrol firmly in its grasp. They wind was so strong that once again they could not leave camp. Fitzgerald wrote: "it was all we could do to keep the tent standing." The day seemed to go on forever. The cold would be torture enough, but the real nightmare was listening to the voice of the wind. The men stayed in their tent as the howling slammed against the thin walls. A gale force at -30°C would cause the temperature to feel more like -62°C. Without food to make energy to heat their bodies and without a fire to keep them warm, all they had was the camp stove. Condensation built up inside the tent, causing droplets of moisture to form and rain down, soaking their bedding, which in turn would reduce the insulating warmth the sleeping blankets could provide. It was a vicious circle.

They cooked up the last of the bacon and bannock and had some tea. It would have been a difficult meal since they knew this would empty their food bag. Only a few dried fish and some tea were remaining, and they still had almost five hundred kilometres to go to get them back to Fort McPherson. Another day had been lost.

ZERO. SATURDAY, JAN 21ST. STRONG GALE UNTIL NOON, MODERATED IN P.M.

The men had within them the instincts and courage that had carried them from the beginning. By 7:45 a.m. they had hitched the remaining dogs and were following their homebound trail. Howling winds battered them, assaulting their ears. Any loose snow was picked up and hurled sideways in frozen pellets that struck the men head on. The leather strips lining the runners on the sled were coated in ice and the dogs were struggling to keep the sleds from careening out of control. It was slow going.

The patrol stopped for an hour to have something hot to drink and then continued, slipping and falling as they tried to run alongside the sleds. Every now and then when the going became too difficult, one of the men would hop on a sled for a ride. By mid-afternoon, the dogs had tired and were unable to continue. They slowed to a walk and just stopped — completely worn out.

Having covered another thirty-two kilometres, they set up their camp nineteen kilometres above the Wind River. Tonight they would kill their third dog. The men were starving and showing signs of hyperthermia. Their bodies were unable to replenish the heat being lost because of the limited food intake. As the drop in their core temperature continued, they began to shiver uncontrollably. Soon mental confusion would be another symptom. They would have no choice but to choke down this heart-breaking meal.

As quickly as they could manage, they pitched the tent, started a fire, and hung wet socks and other sodden gear to dry. Thankfully, the wind had decreased and it was a calm night, but still they leaned as close to the fire as they could, trying to take in all the heat possible. It was time to kill another dog. One was culled from the pack, taken away from the rest, and shot.

Another member of the patrol was dead. Pieces of dog meat were given to the pack and were gulped down. The dogs did not refuse, knowing instinctively that they needed whatever was being offered for survival.

Whoever was on cooking duty skinned the carcass and added the meat to a pot of water. The men probably ate in silence. Staring into the flames of the fire, they may have been thinking of other things, anything to get their minds off the situation and what they were eating. Maybe when they were out on their trail next they would meet a group of Aboriginal people or a trapper who would be able to supply them with food. If they were lucky they might see a moose they could shoot to feed themselves and their dogs. Had they brought along a snare, they could also have set it for a fox or other small animal.

The weather changed. The northern lights began their performance and the stars blurred. Another northern legend tells that Aurora Borealis means "fox fire." The Arctic fox is known to be a confident and fearless animal and it changes the colour of its coat to match the season. In the heart of winter, its coat is as white as the snow that covers its home. According to the legend, the fox brings the dancing lights by sweeping his tail across the snow, sending it skyward into the heavens.[2]

If only the men could see the white-coated fox living near their camp. As the sky cleared the temperature began to plummet. By morning it was -46°C.

ELEVEN
The Struggle Continues

There's a land where the mountains are nameless,
And the rivers all run God knows where;
There are lives that are erring and aimless,
And deaths that just hang by a hair ...[1]

50 BELOW. SUNDAY, JAN. 22ND. VERY MISTY WITH SLIGHT SW WIND.

Their day began as the sky was barely holding its light. It was 7:45 a.m. when they started on the trail again. The mist was thick. It permeated every possible space, blotting out any features that might have signalled danger. That, combined with the condensation from the laboured breathing of the dogs, made it almost impossible to see a metre in front of them. It would have been easy to wander off into oblivion, had the narrow, rugged canyon walls not been keeping them contained. If the extreme cold wasn't a sufficient problem, the winds and snowfall from the previous days had all but obliterated the outbound trail they had fought so hard to make. Conditions were brutal.

It was dangerous to send a trailblazer out ahead, so the patrol slowly made their way along the river, which was in overflow once again. Both men and dogs struggled as they sloshed through the frigid water. The Mounties began to sweat from weakness, causing their clothing to almost freeze on their bodies. They had to stop for tea and build a fire. There was no other choice.

The Struggle Continues

The dogs collapsed in an exhausted heap while the men tended to a fire. Steam rose from their damp clothing and combined with the mist and their breath. Holding mugs of hot tea in shaking painful hands, they sipped the comforting liquid, feeling its warmth ease their parched and raw throats. They may have wanted to just lie down by the fire and give up, but they didn't. Tossing snow on the flames, they roused the dogs and set out again, this time at a walk. They had almost nothing left to keep them going.

Travelling through the overflow erased any snowshoe or paw prints that might have patterned the snow on the river had it been totally frozen. No one would know they had been through the area. Nature was winning. Day by day she was eliminating any evidence that the patrol had been making its way along her waterways and eroding their life's energy. Options for the patrol's safe return were rapidly vanishing.

Throughout the day they scanned the landscape with weary eyes, looking for any signs of life. Surely there must be a ptarmigan, or a fox, or, best yet, a caribou in the vicinity. Their gun was ready just in case something wandered into their path. However, this would be highly unlikely since the already brutal temperature was continuing to fall. It reached a low of -64°C.

They were finally off the river and travelling alongside the bank, but the punishing winds that had blown for the past two days had filled in the trail they had so strenuously broken on their outward journey. This was not normal; frequently trails will hold up for weeks on end.

At 4:00 p.m. they stopped. They were now eight kilometres down the Big Wind River, and they had managed another twenty-seven kilometres, which was a testament to their endurance. When the men unharnessed the dogs they dropped onto the snow, dead beat. Then it was time to set up camp. Fitzgerald noted in his diary that Carter's fingers were badly frozen. It must have been agonizing for Carter to attend to the camp chores in this frostbitten condition. His fingers were starting to blacken from lack of circulation. To save them he would have had to slowly thaw them in warm water — in temperatures of -64°C that was nearly impossible.

Another dog was taken from the pack and made into a meal for both men and dogs. It was a sad and terrible end to another day for this doomed patrol. They sat and ate, then lit their pipes, staring into the burning flames. The four men, together yet alone in their thoughts, were most likely feeling empty and grim. Did they think of family at home? Maybe they were too tired to think. Did they wonder why they had ever signed up? Conversations about the reasons for the patrols and the reasons the Royal Northwest Mounted Police were first envisioned seemed so long ago. These men were trained and sent to the remote regions to protect others, and here they were, in dire need of help themselves. Would a rescue come in time? A heaviness hung in the air.

64 BELOW. MONDAY, 23RD JAN. MISTY WITH STRONG HEADWIND.

They had just lost another day, a day they couldn't afford to lose. A day where they perhaps might have met someone and received some help or at the very least, been able to travel another thirty or so kilometres, bringing them closer to home. It was not to be. They stayed in their tent listening to nature's wailing.

56 BELOW. TUESDAY, JAN. 24TH. STRONG S WIND WITH VERY HEAVY MIST.

They just couldn't get a break. At 7:30 a.m. they headed out into the mist with the remaining dogs. By this time the patrol was feeling the extreme debilitating effects of poor nutrition. Scurvy, caused by lack of vitamin C, was also contributing to their malaise and lethargy, as well as compromising their circulation, which, in turn, affected the ability to keep themselves warm. Still they struggled on.

After travelling nine exhausting kilometres, they were met with "open water" on the river. A devastating discovery that was made worse when Constable Taylor plunged up to his waist in the frigid running water, and Carter up to his hips. They had to stop for the day and build a fire quickly to get both men dry. Both were suffering from extreme bouts of uncontrollable shivering and in danger of hypothermia while the fire was being built. It was only 11:00 a.m. and they could not continue. Another setback.

Wispy smoke rose from the flames. Hands needed to be thawed and water boiled for tea. Their physical shape was deteriorating rapidly, and without proper food they had to make sure they kept hydrated. It is amazing that the men persevered and continued each day. It must have seemed as if they had been moving along this frozen landscape forever, lost in a world so unforgiving and harsh.

Carter and Taylor's clothes were hung to dry by the flames and it didn't take long for them to scorch in the heat. They had to be careful not to let the clothes ignite, since the wind continued to blow forcefully, sending the clothing dangerously close to the fire. The wind chill made breathing painful. Lungs ached. The dogs huddled together for warmth, but some were showing signs of illness. Ice now frosted their matted fur, indicating that the dogs were also losing precious heat. They had been on the trail for thirty-four days at this point and still had many days more to go.

Once the sky darkened, they knew it was time for the inevitable, and pulled a sleeping dog from the heap of dark fur. The husky, with head hung low, followed his master. Soon scarlet life ebbed out of the dying dog. In a way, it was similar to what was happening to the "Scarlet Police." Life was ebbing out of them as well and they were in fact dying a very slow death themselves.

Fitzgerald wrote: "Cold intense with all the open water. Killed another dog and all hands made good meal on dog meat." They made the best of what they had and that was all they could do. After piling wood on the flames to keep the dogs somewhat warm, the men crawled into the tent and wrapped themselves in their damp sleeping blankets as tightly as they could. The thin fabric of the tent shuddered with each northern blast. It would be another stormy night with the wailing and moaning of the wind.

53 BELOW. WEDNESDAY, JAN 25TH.

In the bitter chill the men went out searching for a place to cross the open water. For two hours they tramped down the river until they found a safe location. They then had to go back and harness the dogs and retrace their steps. By noon they were eight kilometres up the Mount Deception trail. They stopped to have hot tea, then continued their struggle in the raw cold. They did find parts of their outbound trail, which was good news, since this saved them the backbreaking work of making a new path. They kept going until 3:30 p.m., then stopped for the day. This time they had covered a good distance of twenty-nine kilometres, which put them about thirty-two kilometres from the mouth of the Peel River. Considering they were down so many dogs, to be able to travel that distance in frightful conditions was remarkable. Fitzgerald wrote that the going had been fairly good.

The patrol set up their camp and made tea. It would soon be time for their evening meal and they would be killing another dog, but they didn't do that right away — it was such a disheartening thing to have to do. Their sole diet now consisted of tea and dog meat, which most certainly would not sustain them with the energy they needed. It was just a matter of time before they would become so weakened that it would be impossible to continue.

It was now eight days since they began heading back to Fort McPherson and in those eight days the patrol had been grounded for two by winds and intense cold. The men had managed to cover just over 160 kilometres, which left another four hundred kilometres. At the rate they were travelling, with an average of twenty-six kilometres a day, they would have another two weeks to go. The fewer the dogs meant the slower their travel time. With only eleven dogs left to feed both the Mounties and the remaining huskies, the prospect looked doubtful, unless they met some-one along their trail that could give them food and help. One of the men

Dog sledding over the Gwitch'in route between Fort McPherson and Dawson was treacherous. Dangers of snow-covered tree wells and rocky boulder outcrops were nature's obstacles that could easily be the cause of serious injury to both men and dogs.

got up and woke a sleeping bundle of fur and once more shattered the stillness with a bullet. They were now down to ten dogs.

The fire hardly made a difference in the -46°C and all must have been at a low ebb that night as they sat in the smoke of the flames. Faces, thin from starvation, looked ghostly in the firelight and dark eyes in sunken sockets probably saw nothing. At least they had survived another day. It was time to head into their tent. All night long the wind would beat the fabric walls. Only sleep would let them escape from the misery.

21 BELOW. THURSDAY, JAN. 26TH. SNOWING WITH VERY HEAVY MIST.

The dogs were harnessed, three on two sleds, and four on the third. The patrol broke camp and were en route by 7:30 a.m. The snow swirled around them as they slowly made their way alongside the river. With the cold temperature freezing the mist, only an outline of the men was visible as they moved along. The space slowly filled in, erasing their presence.

The scene was one of whiteness with the vastness of the sky and a curtain of drifting snow. They crunched along on snowshoes that weakened with each step. That was another concern. Their snowshoes had become brittle in the extreme cold. They could not survive without them and so they carefully trudged onward. After four hours they stopped for hot tea and to rest. The men might have thought of the early days of the patrol when they had a lunch at midday, however, on day thirty-six, there was nothing more than tea, and even that supply was becoming low. Soon water would be their only source of hydration.

The snow continued to fall and for three hours they slogged though the rapidly growing accumulation, trying to get around open water that once again was running over the icy river. The extra effort was using precious energy, energy they just couldn't afford to waste.

At 3:30 p.m. they quit. They simply could not continue, but that still didn't eliminate the camp set-up tasks. With frozen hands they set to work. Every motion was exhausting, but they had no choice if they wanted to survive. Just the very fact they did continue showed they still carried hope. Most likely it was forlorn hope, but hope nonetheless. Fitzgerald wrote: "Going very heavy in deep snow, and all hands and dogs getting weak." It was evident that the men were deteriorating, as were their canine companions. They had only covered thirteen kilometres.

Wet clothes were steaming by the campfire while the snow fell. The great stillness of the North was with them. Did they fear the stillness? Maybe they did, maybe they didn't, but they were well aware that the Aboriginal people who lived in the harsh Northern reaches did have fear of the spirits that lived among them, and believed that there were consequences for negative actions.

The Inuit, whom Fitzgerald and members of the Fort McPherson and Herschel Island detachments had been sent to protect, had many legends that were shared with the Mounties during the dark, cold winter months. These legends helped the people make sense of their world, strengthened their sense of community, and provided a common understanding, giving meaning to life. Legends were a way of providing moral guidance.

The Inuit were respectful people, perhaps as a result of living in such an inhospitable climate, and they had great regard for all living things. For one thing, they approached the killing of animals with thoughtful care, sometimes verging on trepidation. They believed that all living things had a spirit or soul and that these spirits lived on after death. They believed that dangers would arise to threaten their very existence, because their traditional diet consisted, in effect, of souls. The belief was that killing an animal was no different than killing a human. Once the *anirniq*, or soul, of the animal is liberated in death, then the soul has the right to take revenge. The spirit will only be placated by the Inuit's performing the right rituals, customs, and obedience in their beliefs.

The Inuit understood that life was fragile, and they lived in a constant awareness of unseen forces. For the Inuit to offend an *anirniq* was to risk extinction. They remained an obedient people, feeling the *anirniit* were all around them, and so had to live with a great respect for all life. By praising the slain animal to others and telling how it had provided food, clothing, and shelter for them, the Inuit believed they would be safe. The *anirniq* would become a figure of influence or respect and in turn this would prevent any disaster that might otherwise have befallen them.[2]

As they themselves struggled to survive, the Mounties may have felt this same type of fear. They may have thought about the myth and wondered about killing the dogs, for them a repugnant act. Feeding the dogs their own kind, an act of cannibalism, it likely made it seem even worse. They knew that as the number of dogs declined, so did their chances of survival. Barely able to put one foot in front of the other, men and dogs were nonetheless now engaged in a race against time.

Were the dogs an *anirniit* travelling with them, following them? If the Inuit legend was true, how might their actions involving the dogs impact the outcome of the race against their own death?

TWELVE
Losing the Race

Things never were looking so black.
But show that you haven't a cowardly streak,
And though you're unlucky you never are weak.
Carry on! Carry on![1]

13 BELOW. FRIDAY, JAN. 27TH. HEAVY SNOWSTORM WITH HEAVY MIST.

The winter patrol just couldn't seem to get a break. The snowstorm was blinding, obscuring the obstacles standing in their way. The trees that lined the river would suddenly appear, just in time to be avoided. Snowshoes sank deeply into the ever increasing layers of snow. Each step was agony, and there was no rhythm to their walking. Weakened by their inadequate diet, they staggered as if they were drunk.

At noon they stopped, had hot tea, and within the hour lurched back out into the blizzard once more. The huskies were very weak and struggled to pull the sleds. Both men and dogs were suffering from laboured breathing. The men's frostbitten patches were peeling, fingers were frozen, and muscles screamed from exertion, yet they managed to cover another seventeen kilometres. At 2:00 p.m. they found the tent belonging to a prospector known as Harry Waugh. This must have been a tremendous relief! Perhaps they would find food for themselves and a stash of dried fish for the dogs.

The need for food was urgent. Had they energy for enthusiasm, this would have quickly turned to dismay, for when they searched the tent for any sign of nourishment there was nothing to be found. It would be another night of dog meat and tea.

A shot rang out, another dog lay dead, and their dinner was soon cooked. Dog bones and parts unfit for human consumption were given to the remaining nine animals. By this time the men's bodies were experiencing bouts of uncontrolled shivering caused by hypothermia. Scurvy added to their general malaise. Their speech was slurred. Foggy thinking would soon follow since they were barely clinging to life. The handwriting in Fitzgerald's diary revealed deterioration in his motor skills. Surely the following day they would get help. They had to meet a tribe of First Nations, or a trapper or prospector who would give them assistance. There must be someone or some large game animal in the vicinity. Living on one meal of dog meat a day would not sustain them.

The red-hot casing of the camp stove gradually dulled. It was the end of another day. That night was a restless night, with Taylor being violently sick. Retching tore apart his already weakened body; his stomach was reacting both to dog meat and exhaustion. Life was ebbing out of him. Outside the tent, the dogs huddled for warmth. The cold was frightful and the huskies were suffering. The dogs had heart and were willing to do as asked, but it wouldn't be long before their bodies shut down, putting an end to what they could pull.

During the night the raging blizzard blew itself out, the sky cleared, and twinkling stars emerged. The clear skies meant there was no cloud insulating this part of the world, which meant decreasing temperatures. There was stillness. Then the northern lights started to dance. Was it *Selamiut*, the Sky Dwellers, lighting torches waiting for the Mounties? It was beginning to seem inevitable that the patrol was on the edge of death.

45 BELOW. SATURDAY, JAN. 28TH. STRONG SOUTH WIND WITH MIST

There was no breakfast. They had stuffed their blankets back into their kits, loaded the gear, and harnessed the remaining dogs, three to a sled, and were heading into a gale-force wind by 7:45 a.m. Throughout the day Richard

Taylor continued to stop to be sick. As to whether he rode in the sled or walked was not recorded in the diary. It must have been the worst day yet for him. Bumping along in a sled, feeling nauseated and being sick, or staggering on snowshoes in the face of a gale, and stopping when he could go no further, seems inconceivable.

At noon they stopped to regain their breath, change their sweat-soaked clothes, add on another layer of clothing, and make a pot of hot tea to drink. After their hour-long break, they headed out again along the banks of the Peel River, breaking trail as they went, since there was very little of their outbound route remaining. The going was excruciatingly difficult. Heavy snow and thick mist had enveloped them all day, hampering their progress. After seven-and-a-half hours they found one of the camps they had made after leaving Fort McPherson, and decided they could go no further.

Starting a fire came first. At -42°C, with the wind chill, the air would have felt more like -55°C, and the dampness from the mist would have made their bones ache. It would be doubtful that the men could have ever felt warm again until they had proper food, but a fire was made nonetheless. Cold was a constant stalker and enemy. They had to dry out their clothing, thaw frozen hands and feet, and make tea. Fitzgerald's diary made no mention of killing a dog, so perhaps they still had meat from the night before to feed the nine dogs and themselves.

The inspector recorded that the patrol covered another nineteen kilometres and that they were now about five kilometres below the Peel River Canyon. Since starting back to Fort McPherson ten days earlier they had travelled a distance of 195 kilometres. But the daily distances were not what the men had hoped to achieve.

Sitting and staring at the fire with dazed eyes, they must have just willed themselves to live, for there was certainly nothing else to keep them going. These men never seemed frightened of taking a chance, but surely by this point fear must have been a constant companion. The motto of the RNWMP was, and still is, "Maintain the right." To do this they had been trained to keep order among those they served. They approached all tasks with discipline and a sense of organization, even to the point of rising at the same time every morning. Fitzgerald doggedly kept his diary and recorded the day-to-day events as he was taught to do. Somehow they still managed to resist the idea that their world was spinning out of control.

20 BELOW. SUNDAY, JAN. 29TH. SNOWING WITH LIGHT NE WIND.

Day followed night, and at 7:30 a.m. they were trying to find and follow their outbound trail. Weakened from hunger, exhaustion, hypothermia, and scurvy, their progress was slow, yet they soldiered on. At noon, they stopped for an hour "break." They had now arrived back at Mountain Creek, and in about a day's time they would be back at the vertical hill, leading to the head of Mountain Creek. With each step they were sinking into almost waist-deep snow. This was too much for the men. At 1:30 p.m. they found an abandoned cabin and stopped.

Once again, if they had hoped to find something left by the previous occupant they were disappointed. The cabin offered shelter, but nothing more. The patrol unloaded the sleds and took their gear inside. Fitzgerald brought his diary up to date and estimated that the patrol had travelled only sixteen kilometres. This was heartbreaking. The daily distance being covered was decreasing, but was understandable now that there were fewer dogs to pull the sleds, severe weather conditions, and men with deteriorating physical strength and endurance. Everything seemed to be against them.

One of them took a dog from the pack. Before long they were eating, but by this time all their stomachs were reacting negatively. Fitzgerald reported that the men and dogs were becoming very weak. For eleven days they had been surviving on dog meat, and in those days they had killed and eaten seven of their dogs. With eight dogs remaining and a distance of roughly 333 kilometres to go, common sense would have told them that they stood no chance of making it back to Fort McPherson alive.

They made the decision that they would leave one of their sleds at the cabin and carry on with two sleds, harnessing four dogs per sled. They also would leave seven dog harnesses behind, a grim reminder of how small their patrol had become.

The forces of nature continued their cruel assault on the struggling men, sending more cold Arctic air down from the polar region. The temperature

Yukon Archives, 007615.

Breaking trail assisted the dogs with as firm footing possible. Much of the region where the patrols passed through are covered with snow for eight months a year. Travelling through the area with dog teams is extremely tough going.

fell sharply to -51°C below under a clear sky. Perhaps the Sky Dwellers were lighting torches once again for the patrol, encouraging them to come along the pathway of lights. The northern lights were pulsating with energy, something they would have liked to have been able to tap. They were beyond exhaustion and would have only wanted to sleep, but even this small comfort was impossible with their stomachs cramping and in spasm.

51 BELOW. MONDAY, JAN. 30TH. FINE WITH LIGHT W WIND.

The men were all feeling ill, yet they had managed to harness the eight dogs to the two sleds and were off again by 7:45 a.m. The going was heavy because of the recent snowfall and the frigid temperature. With their old trail having filled in, they were having to break a new pathway as best they could. This time the trailbreaker did not venture out in front, for if he did he could have easily wandered off to lie down and rest and been lost. Two men walked, while two rested. The dogs had no reprieve and they just continued to pull.

The cold was beyond comprehension. The skin on their drawn faces was beginning to fall off in patches as frostbite continued its attack. The men were just husks of their former selves. It was remarkable they were even able to put one snowshoe in front of the other. They spent their noon rest hour retching into the snow. Doubled over in agony, they were reacting to the dog meat they were compelled to eat. Fitzgerald wrote that he felt these bouts of spasms were due to eating the dog's liver.

They carried on.

At 3:15 p.m. they stopped at the foot of the big hill on Mountain Creek. With the daylight fading and their depleted state, they needed to rest. In retrospect, it had not been a bad day on the trail, since they somehow managed to cover twenty-two more kilometres. They set up camp and built a fire. They were cold and miserable and in a desolate place with night closing in around them. The orange flames crackled and sparks shot off into the air. They gathered as close as they could to the flames, trying to absorb the heat and its comfort, yet with caution because of frostbite pain. By now the men were unable to keep their own body temperature up since for days there had been no fat in their diets to create energy. They shivered and shook, adding more pain to already weakened muscles.

They cooked some dog meat and tea for dinner. Maybe they thought of the peaceful nights at the outset of the patrol, when they were eating bacon and beans and bannock with dried fruit. Maybe they thought about the Christmas feast and the New Year's feast they had missed at Fort McPherson. Maybe they thought about home and meals shared with family. Maybe they were beyond thinking.

A moon rose over the mountain and cast its silver light on the ice of Mountain Creek. It looked like a gentle and kind world, however, it was anything but, and the men knew it. They crawled into damp sleeping blankets and continued to shiver.

45 BELOW IN A.M. TUESDAY, JAN. 31ST. 62 BELOW IN P.M.

It was day forty-two on the trail, twelve days after they should have arrived in Dawson City. The men must have wondered if their whereabouts were being questioned. Maybe a patrol had been sent out to look for them. The great hill of Mountain Creek loomed in front of them, and by 7:15 a.m. they were ready to attempt it. They harnessed all dogs to one sled, and pulled and hauled with the animals to get the gear up the hill. The incline was a steep and continuous climb for two-and-a-half kilometres. Conditions were treacherous. How they managed to do this while ravaged with sickness and fatigue gives testimony to their hidden reserves. And they had to repeat the trip up the hill. Once one sled had been hauled up the slope, they stumbled and fell back down, only to fight their way up again with the second sled. Finally, the physical obstacle had been overcome and sleds, dogs, and men had made it to the top of Mountain Creek. They took a break for an hour, then carried on. They must have just wanted to lie down and sleep. To do that, however, would have been certain death.

The kilometres seemed endless as they plodded along the treacherous terrain. The patrol did manage to find parts of their old trail still viable, but for the most part they were trudging through heavy snowfall, breaking the path again. The next turnoff would be the Caribou River. At 4:15 p.m. Fitzgerald wrote that they stopped six-and-a-half kilometres from the river. What the patrol didn't take into consideration was that they were following their outbound trail, the one that had taken them off the normal patrol route. When the Mounties met Esau George and his people, they had already added many more kilometres to their travels than necessary, and by retracing their steps now, they were adding further distance to their homebound journey. In the mental fog in which they were now moving, this oversight had not occurred to any of them.

Thoroughly exhausted, they still had to set up camp. They had some dog meat and ate that for supper. The agony of their frostbite continued, their frozen nerve endings thawing into fresh agony. The temperature had dropped to -52°C. Fitzgerald described the day as "Going heavy, travelled part of the time on our old trail, but it was filled in. Skin peeling off our faces and parts of the body and lips all swollen and split. I suppose this is caused by feeding on dog meat. Everybody feeling the cold very much, for want of proper food." Again, the fire did little to warm the physically drained and very weary Mounties. After so many weeks in the punishing elements, they all resembled corpses more than men, their features hollowed out by privation and extreme suffering.

51 BELOW IN A.M. WEDNESDAY, FEB. 1ST. FINE WITH STRONG SW WIND.

How they got up and on the trail by 7:30 a.m. on that first day of February is baffling, yet they were back on duty. The strong wind would have made the temperature feel colder than -46°C. Exertion in such a weakened condition would have caused excessive sweating, which again would freeze against their skin. The thin layers of ice on their face, formed by the moisture in their breath, crackled with each painful inhale and exhale. During the day, however, the temperature began to climb. With an increase in temperature the surface conditions began to deteriorate and the snow accumulation, as described by Fitzgerald, became "very heavy."

At noon they stopped to rest their worn-out bodies. Hearts pounded, as their breathing gradually slowed. As if to mock them, the sun shone, and it seemed the forces of nature smiled on the Mounties. Temperatures continued to rise. After their hour break they headed slowly off again for three more hours. Every step was more painful than the last. For each man, the focus was on putting one foot in front of the other. At 4:00 p.m. the patrol was at the start of Caribou Born Mountain. They set up camp to dry their clothes, melt ice for the dogs, and make tea for themselves. Since they were out of dog meat, another was culled from the pack and killed. This job must have been so difficult, even though they had no choice.

Fitzgerald wrote: "this makes eight dogs we have killed and we have eaten most of them and fed what dried fish [was left] to the dogs." The dogs were getting a mixed diet of dog meat on some nights and whatever dried fish remained. That day on the trail was a good one. They had covered twenty-six kilometres, a remarkable feat considering the obstacles they were facing. It was quite a day contending with weather since the temperature had risen an incredible fifty degrees! And it was still climbing. With rising temperatures came a concern about mist. It was creeping stealthily towards the group of men and dogs.

THIRTEEN
Duty to the Death

And so they sweep the solitudes, free men from all the earth;
And so they sentinel the wood, the wilds that know their worth;
And so they scour the startled plains and mock at hurt and pain
And read their Crimson Manual, and find their duty plain.[1]

7 ABOVE IN A.M. THURSDAY, FEB. 2ND. FINE IN THE A.M., VERY MISTY ON THE MOUNTAIN.
The Mounties broke camp, and by 7:00 a.m. they were trudging along
though the heavy waist-high snow and heavy mist, which seemed to fill
every space around them. Nearly blinded by the fog, and disoriented
because of starvation, sickness, and exhaustion, they became lost in the suffocating whiteness. They stopped for an hour to regain their bearings, but
unable to do so, they camped on the mountain at 3:30 p.m. The men were
nearly spent both mentally and physically, their thinking processes almost
at a standstill. Confusion was taking control. They were in the most difficult
and rugged terrain between Fort McPherson and Dawson City. This was an
area that could easily swallow intruders, and they still had kilometres and
kilometres to go until the trail became easier. They had managed to cross
one of the first mountains, but were now back on Caribou Born Mountain.

On their outbound journey, the men with their fifteen dogs had taken
a full eight days to cover this area. Back then they were in good health,

had proper food, and fresh dogs willing to pull loads. They had a trail-blazer who could break the trail for the patrol. They also had met a group of First Nations who guided them back onto the correct route to Dawson City. Now they were once again lost, this time on the glacier of a trail-less mountain, with all landmarks or guiding signs invisible. To make matters worse, the temperature was starting to fall sharply.

But this didn't cause them to give up. They just checked on the dogs and began their tasks. Building a fire was just something so routine that the men just did it. They set up their tent, heated some dog meat, and made tea. Fitzgerald wrote in his diary that they had travelled sixteen kilometres. It was another Herculean achievement.

They managed to rest and rise the next morning.

26 BELOW. FRIDAY, FEB. 3RD. MISTY IN A.M. CLEAR IN P.M. STRONG NE WIND.

By 7:45 they had packed up, harnessed the remaining dogs and continued their attempt on the mountain. Eternally optimistic, Fitzgerald wrote:

> crossed the mountain by 1:30 p.m. and camped on Trail Creek at the mouth of the small creek. Killed another dog tonight and had to feed some of it to the dogs as we have no dried fish. Men and dogs very thin and weak and cannot travel far. We have travelled about 200 miles on dog meat and have still about 100 miles to go, but I think we will make it alright but will have only 3 or 4 dogs left.

The patrol had made it another twenty-two-and-a-half kilometres in the six hours. The successful crossing over Caribou Born Mountain was a huge achievement for them, even though they had no energy to celebrate the feat. It was day forty-five, and if they could continue at the pace they set today, without any additional obstacles, they might arrive within a week. They needed the weather to remain "moderate," meaning in the -20°C range. Not too warm, which would bring more mist, but not in the extreme lows, which would bring a very real threat of freezing to death.

The Mounties' endurance and discipline was incredible. They made camp once more. Setting a match to a handful of dry twigs, one man nursed the little flicker of flame until it came to life, then knelt in the snow and blew gently while the branches steamed. He patiently waited until the smoldering wood finally caught. Smoke rose into the air, and he added more wood onto the growing flames. Soon a crackling sound and the smell of burning wood spread throughout the valley. Perhaps someone would smell this and come to see who was out in the wilderness. After all, it was still early afternoon.

While sitting around the campfire in the light of the day, they could see that the cold and starvation had pulled the shrunken tissue on their faces, stretching the skin tightly across their cheekbones, and, in some places, peeling it back, exposing raw flesh, which was turning black. Yet the inspector continued to hold out hope. He wrote that he thought they could make it if the weather would cooperate. But nature had something else in mind for this group, who, although struggling for their lives, still seemed so strong.

The sky remained clear and luckily no new snow fell, which would have been cause for another type of torture. Maybe the men noticed the temperature plummet again, or maybe they were too numb, wrapped instead in thoughts or making perfunctory conversation to keep their spirits up. As dusk turned to darkness a thin pale curtain of northern lights hung in the sky. A campfire, crystal-clear skies with the northern lights, and the almost inaudible gurgle of the creek's running water under the ice made it seem like a magical evening. But they were oblivious to their surroundings.

The tranquil scene changed when a wind started to blow. The tent shook and shuddered as blasting Arctic gusts made the assault. Did this awake the men? Or were they too tired to notice?

52 BELOW. SATURDAY, FEB. 4TH. FINE WITH STRONG S.E. WIND.

Despite forceful winds attempting to hold them back, they managed to get on the trail by 7:45 a.m. and follow the bank of Trail Creek. The wind chill would have made the temperature feel more like -87°C. They could barely breathe the frigid Arctic air. The risk of hypothermia was great and the energy required to continue was enormous. They just didn't have it. Labouring for over seven hours, and sweating alongside each other from sheer weakness, they had managed to cover twelve kilometres. This was not a good day, and, if minimal distances like this continued, the Mounties would not make it home.

Fitzgerald wrote in his diary that the men all suffered "very much with the cold." What they experienced, in their condition, must have been beyond human endurance. He penned that the going was very heavy and that they had managed to make "eight miles" down Trail Creek. They still were kilometres away from the Peel River, the river that would take them back to Fort McPherson.

At 3:00 p.m. they set up camp, and even though another day was coming to an end, there was still a lot to be done. Maybe if they had some good luck, the following day would be kinder and gentler, with warmer temperatures and an easier trail to follow.

The fire was burning, and perhaps they just stared at it, frozen in silence. Faces blue from frostbite and lack of circulation hid the dark circles under their eyes. The hardship they were suffering was terrible, but they were trained not to become unhinged and to carry on with orders, even if it meant risking their lives in the process.

There may have been a hint of snow in the dark clouds that grew overhead, but the temperature showed no sign of warming up. The wind continued to blow. This was not what they had hoped would come their way.

48 BELOW. SUNDAY, FEB. 5TH. FINE WITH STRONG S.E. WIND.

By 7:15 a.m. the patrol had managed to rouse themselves from their sleeping blankets, harness the dead-tired dogs to the sleds, and head off towards the Peel River. The wind raced over the surface of the frozen creek, bringing with it loose ice granules and snow that vigorously attacked them. Frozen particles filled their eyes and froze in sharp clumps on their eyelashes. The ice crystals hissed in their ears and stole their breath time and again. Conditions were dreadful. To continue Mounties had to get to the other side of the waterway. It was during this crossing that disaster struck. Fitzgerald broke through the ice and plunged into the freezing water. The shock of the frigid water hit his emaciated body, propelling him into a world of extreme pain. He struggled to reach the other side, but not quickly enough time to avoid freezing one foot.

Uncontrollable bouts of shaking threatened to tear his body apart. His heart raced to circulate blood and his embattled being veered between consciousness and unconsciousness. The latter would easily have been preferable to what he was experiencing. His body was not of much use by this time, as his internal system was beyond compromised. Timing was critical if he was to avoid hypothermia.

It was not a simple process. One of the men grabbed the now dull axe and hacked wood from a nearby tree while the others gathered brush to get a fire going. They were all keenly aware that Fitzgerald was at risk of death. Despite their weariness, the men soon had the inspector in dry clothes and wrapped in a blanket, but this catastrophe put an end to their travel for that day. They had only covered another thirteen kilometres. The chance of reaching Fort McPherson in the seven days as hoped was quickly diminishing.

One of the men took another starving, exhausted dog from the pack and killed it.

Constables Taylor and Kinney were reaching the end of their endurance. The younger men were in a desperate situation. They had almost run out of reserve and it was becoming clear that their days were limited. Even the freshly slaughtered dog would not alleviate their hunger. Each of the men had by now punched new holes in their belts, and their ribs and hipbones were beginning to stand out sharply.

Fitzgerald reported in his diary; "have only five dogs more and can only go a few miles a day, everybody breaking out on the body and skin peeling off." This was Fitzgerald's last entry in his log.

For forty-seven days he had documented their trials. He had written where they were, recorded daily temperatures, noted weather conditions and distances covered, and described their experiences. Although this was his last entry, it did not mark the end of the patrol, and they would continue the next day on their struggle down the Trail River towards the homestretch to the mighty Peel River.

On the morning of February 6, Fitzgerald, Carter, Taylor, and Kinney left their wretched little oasis of a camp, heading towards the final run down the Peel River. The two sleds were loaded and the remaining dogs pulling. They were now roughly 112 kilometres from Fort McPherson.

The tormented group stumbled along the trail, and the worn-out dogs pulled the sleds as best they could. Brittle branches from the scraggly trees that lined the trail reached out as if to halt the men's stumbling progress. This part of the trail was full of turns and climbs and the trees were laden with snow, just waiting to dump loads on the bowed heads below. It was a cold and white world. The men moved ever so slowly on shaking legs, inching closer to their destination. One more step, just one more step, and on it went. They were the example of that thinness of margin by which human life is sustained. Hope and the call of duty were what kept them going.

FEBRUARY 20, 1911, DAWSON CITY, YUKON TERRITORIES

After being paid out by Fitzgerald on Sunday, January 1, 1911, Esau George continued to roam the area with his group. They hunted around Hart River and towards the end of February headed into town. When he reached Dawson, George proceeded to the detachment and reported to the officer in command. It was customary for Native people to visit the NWMP when they arrived into town, a practice that enabled the officers to get first-hand information from the Yukon wilderness. George asked about Inspector Fitzgerald's patrol and was surprised when he heard that they had not shown up in Dawson City. The commanding officer became concerned and began to ask some questions. Since there was no telegraph communication between Fort McPherson and Dawson City, there was no way to see if the patrol had for some reason returned to McPherson. This was the first suggestion of problems. He would need to make a detailed report and he carefully took down Esau George's statement.

George described how his people had met the patrol on the night of December 26, and how the patrol at that point was already several kilometres off the normal Dawson to Fort McPherson route. He explained that after guiding the patrol for five days and getting them back on the correct trail, he was paid $24, then left the group near the mouth of Mountain Creek. George told the winter patrol that they were fifteen days outside of Dawson City and that they should arrive on or around

January 15. The Native guide also reported how he had been willing to stay with the patrol and bring them to Dawson, but that this offer had been turned down. Carter had told George that he knew the trail, but the guide was not so sure he did and did not feel it was his place to say so.

He pointed out to the officer at the detachment that Carter had done the patrol only once before and several years prior, and also that it had been in the opposite direction, from Dawson to Fort McPherson. Esau George noted that the terrain looks very different from each direction. The Native continued that he thought the dogs were in good enough shape to make the trip and that he thought they were good dogs. He remarked that although the Mounties had but a single .30-30 rifle, finding game during the winter would not be easy for them. Had the patrol taken a shotgun, they would have likely found and been able to kill ptarmigan or other small animals for food.

Esau George carried on with his statement, and it was the next piece of information that raised the commanding officer's concern even further. George said that Carter, "… also had a map, but I do not think it was any good as one creek that I knew was not shown on it."[2] Fitzgerald also had a compass with him, however, if the map wasn't accurate, the compass would be of little help.[3]

George also commented that while the Mounties had snowshoes, they were not very good because they were too small and would sink into the snow with each step, making walking very difficult. The more the Native spoke, the more concerned the officer in command became. Fitzgerald and Carter were considered northern men, seasoned veterans of this inhospitable land. They had lived in the North for years and had patrolled and been posted in the regions as remote as Herschel Island. There had never been a problem on the winter patrols in the past. This was unsettling news.

Around this time, another group of First Nations reported that they had been hunting in the Peel River district and they had not seen the Mounties pass through that area, either.[4] If the patrol had been on the right trail, they would have met the group. A second band, this one from the Hart River divide, had also not seen any sign of the patrol. The news travelled around the detachment and concerns for the safety of Fitzgerald and his men heightened.

In anticipation of approval from Regina, A.F. Synder, the superintendent commanding "B" Division, sent a wire to Forty Mile for Corporal W.J.D. Dempster to report immediately to Dawson with his dogs. Synder then began writing to the commissioner of the Royal Northwest Mounted Police in Regina, Saskatchewan.

> Sir,
>
> Fort Macpherson [*sic*] Indians arrived here to-day. One of the party was with Fitzgerald to the head of Mountain creek where he was discharged on New Year's Day. Indians state Mountain creek twenty days from Dawson, easy travelling. Another band from Hart River Divide where patrol should pass saw nothing of them. Latter Indians nine days from that point to Dawson.[5]

The message continued that Snyder was organizing a patrol but would wait for approval and any special instructions.

Superintendent Snyder sent the message, which reached Regina just before the telegraph wire went dead. He would not, however, be receiving a quick response, since unbeknownst to both Snyder and the commissioner in Regina, with no communications coming in, Dawson City was now as isolated as Fort McPherson. This meant that even if the patrol had come in, their arrival could not be announced to Regina.

PART TWO

---◆---

Dempster:
In Search of the Lost Patrol

FOURTEEN
Iron Man of the Trail

In selecting Cpl Dempster to lead this patrol, Superintendent Synder discussed with him the best men to accompany him. He knew that Dempster, in addition to being a well seasoned trailman, was hardy and courageous and with a knowledge of the country between Dawson and Fort MacPherson [sic] that would prove invaluable.[1]

Since the superintendent had not heard from his commissioner, he tried to send the message to Regina over the United States transmission line. The second long-distance wire also failed since the wind and snowstorms that had plagued Fitzgerald's men had also disabled these cable wires. This must have been a source of frustration for the worried superintendent. He was not hearing a reply from Regina, and since there was no communication as far north as Fort McPherson he was unable to contact that detachment either. All he could do was wonder — where was Fitzgerald's winter patrol?

A full fifty-one days had passed since the patrol had been seen alive on the trail. In the best case scenario, Fitzgerald and the men would have turned around and headed back to Fort McPherson, but the only way to determine that was to send a patrol out from Dawson to search for them. Snyder needed to get an answer to his message, and, once granted approval, a new patrol would be dispatched. In the meantime he continued making preparations for the search. He was confident Corporal William John Duncan "Jack" Dempster would locate the whereabouts of Fitzgerald's patrol.[2]

Dempster had been on the winter patrol from Dawson City to Fort McPherson several times and was the logical choice to be in charge. Along with Dempster, Snyder chose Constable J.F. Fyfe, Ex-Constable F. Turner, and Native guide Charles Stewart. Dempster, Fyfe, and Turner were members of the patrol in 1909, and Charles Stewart had also accompanied the Mounties on several trips to Fort McPherson.[3] The four men would be taking three sleds, each one pulled by five dogs. Dempster's patrol would have the benefit of the heavier loads of food and camping gear being freighted by horse to the head of Twelve Mile, a distance of almost one hundred kilometres, rather than having the dogs pull fully loaded sleds right from the start. This would allow the rescue patrol to "get their trail legs."

The Dempster relief patrol (left-right): former Constable F. Turner, Corporal Jack Dempster, and Constable J.F. Fyfe, sent to search for Inspector Fitzgerald and his men.

Dempster was known as "The Iron Man of the Trail" because of his legendary dogsled patrols from Dawson City to Fort McPherson. He had completed the 670-kilometre trip ten times in four years. The trail he followed was one shown to him by the Gwich'in people who had learned the route from their ancestors.[4] By the time of the 1911 search Dempster had been policing the North for thirteen years and knew the Yukon and Peel River systems like the back of his hand. If anyone could find the missing patrol it would be Dempster.

He was ready with his dogs but authorization had not yet arrived from Regina. The commissioner there had sent a wire in response to Snyder on February 21 and another on the 24th, but because the telegraph poles and wires had not been repaired, the urgent messages did not get through. It was not until February 27, a full week after Snyder had sent the wire to Regina, that he finally received the approval he had been expecting. "Send out a patrol" was the message, and immediately the superintendent forwarded instructions to Corporal Dempster:

> You will leave to-morrow morning for a patrol over the Fort McPherson trail, to locate the whereabouts of Insp. Fitzgerald's party. Indians from McPherson reported him on New Year's Day at Mountain creek and their travelling from Mountain creek about 20 days to Dawson.
>
> I understand that at Hart River Divide no matter what route he took he would have to cross this divide. I think it would be advisable to make for this point and take up his trail from there.
>
> I cannot give you any specific instructions: you will have to be guided by circumstances and your own judgment, bearing in mind that nothing is to stand in your way until you have got into touch with this party.
>
> Keep me posted when opportunity occurs of your movement, even to the extent of sending a courier in [if] one is procurable, that is, provided you have anything [of] importance to report."[5]

Dempster and his patrol were packed and ready. The heavily laden horse wagon left ahead of the patrol and would help for the first leg of the journey. The trail from Dawson City began thirty kilometres down the Yukon River, at the mouth of the Twelve Mile River, now called the Chandindu River. From there the men would mush 105 kilometres up the Twelve Mile River, at which point the route would cross over the Seela Pass and bring them to the Blackstone River. While heading along the river they would cross the divide to the Little Hart River. The Dempster patrol would follow this river down to Waugh Creek. Turning up the creek, they would then cross another divide to the Little Wind and the Wind Rivers. Once striking the Peel River, the men would take the cutoff to Mountain Creek and across a sixty-seven-kilometre portage to the Trail River. At the junction of the Trail and Peel Rivers they would head along the Peel for the last 113 kilometres into Fort McPherson.[6] The route was well-known to both Dempster and his guide. The patrol headed out. Their journey would not be easy.

By late February the weather was in transition and the Dempster relief patrol would be plagued with overflow water and brutally cold temperatures.

The relief patrol stands outside the Dawson City Detachment just minutes prior to heading out on the search for Fitzgerald and his men.

Any signs of the Fitzgerald patrol trail would be a challenge to not only find but to follow. They had supplies for thirty days, and, with their heavy gear for the first part of patrol being hauled in by Constable R. Brackett, the driver of the horse, they would not only be amply provisioned but would also be able to conserve their energy for later in the trip. Brackett would accompany the relief party for about forty-eight miles (seventy-seven kilometres) out from Dawson. The men didn't expect any difficulty in reaching Fort McPherson, where they hoped they would find the winter patrol alive and well.

MARCH 1. LEFT TWELVE MILE ROADHOUSE AT 8 A.M., ARRIVED AT POWER HOUSE AT 3:30 P.M., AND LOADED TOBOGGANS READY FOR EARLY MORNING START.[7]

At 8:00 a.m., on a very brisk March 2 morning, and in a temperature of -15°C, Dempster's patrol was on their way. By this time their dogs had their trail legs and were adept at pulling the heavy toboggans, with their masters calling out commands. As the day progressed, the temperature began to rise. Twelve Mile River flooded with overflow. The patrol struggled through the slush and spray from the toboggans, becoming soaked in the process. The moccasins they were wearing were frozen stiff, and the men had to stop to change into dry footwear. Frostbite at the early stage in the search would be disastrous. Towards the later part of the day, water became less of a problem as they headed towards the first glacier they would have to climb.

For about three kilometres the lower part of the glacier ice was like glass, and the dogs had a difficult time trying to gain their footing as they struggled up the slight up-grade. Even with sharp claws to dig into the ice, they were sliding back as fast as they tried to move forward. Legs were sprawling in all directions, and, with the force of gravity exerting pressure on them, the approximately four hundred kilogram weight of the sleds pulled both dogs and their loads down the incline. One of the men had the bright idea of using the axe to cut footholds in the ice. The men gradually worked their way up the side of the glacier, creating steps, and hauling the heavy sleds, giving as much assistance to the dogs as they could.

Since the light was fading, the Mounties decided to make camp. They would face the glacier again the following morning. It was only when they stopped that they realized Constable Turner's feet were frostbitten and he was in severe pain. He had said nothing, but continued to climb and attended to setting up camp as if all was normal. Nothing could be done to alleviate his pain and so nothing was done.

Dempster's patrol performed the same camp tasks as had Fitzgerald's winter patrol. Dogs had to be checked, the tent set up, meals made, and, of course, the fire built. Food was put into the pot and smells of the evening meal wafted into the night air.

This night was their third on the trail. They sat around the campfire just as patrols do and they chatted. These men, however, were not on a normal patrol — they were really doing investigative work. Timing was critical. If Fitzgerald's patrol was in trouble, each hour spent in the sub-zero temperatures could mean the difference between life and death. They were going to cover as much trail as possible and as fast as possible.

With Dempster's knowledge of the trail and his keen awareness of the obstacles they might face, he was confident his patrol would locate the missing men alive. This would be a remarkable achievement since travelling at this time of year would present challenges, plus the fact that they were searching a massive area.

However, Dempster not only had his own experience of the North, but also that of Charlie Stewart, a Native guide, who was also an important member of the patrol. Dempster never went on patrol without a guide from one of local First Nations. The four likely discussed what could have happened to Fitzgerald and what areas would most likely be the ones to produce any clues as to their whereabouts. Their first hope was that the Mounties had turned around and made their way safely back to Fort McPherson. Interestingly, the search for the Fitzgerald's winter patrol wasn't the first time the NWMP had been sent out looking for lost people held in the grip of the North.

———◆———

Ten years earlier, at exactly the same spot where Dempster and his patrol were absorbing the heat from their campfire, there had been another search party. This one was led by an ex-British Army officer and seven-year veteran of the NWMP. Alick Pennycuick had patrolled the Yukon at the turn of the century, and, in 1900, he was sent to investigate the disappearance of three wealthy travellers who were making their way down the Yukon Trail. They had vanished without a trace in the snow-laden land. Suspecting foul play, Alick Pennycuick had his eye on a suspect named George O'Brian, but without proof O'Brian and his dog continued on with their daily life.

Pennycuick and another officer devised a systematic search of the one hundred square kilometres along the river trail. It was in the depths of winter, and Pennycuick had his trusted dog team with him. While combing the area, one of the sled dogs began to paw at the snow. With snow flying, it dug down through the layers, and suddenly Pennycuick could see that the dog had found a patch of frozen blood. The Mountie had a hunch that the blood the dog had discovered was not that of an animal, and decided to send for O'Brian's own dog. Once the husky was brought to the scene, it sniffed the frozen blood. Pennycuick turned the dog loose and followed it to an abandoned riverside campsite. It was there, after six weeks of searching, that he began to turn up evidence that would pin the crime on O'Brian.

At the campsite there was charred clothing, bits of a moccasin, and cartridge cases. Out on the river Pennycuick found a spot where there had been a disturbance in the ice and he suspected this might be a place where a hole had been chopped and bodies stuffed through to dispose of them. Upon further investigation, the officer made the grisly discovery of a piece of human skull and a bullet embedded in a broken tooth. Pennycuick had the evidence he needed. He went to speak with O'Brian.

Later, during the spring melt, the bodies of the three wealthy travellers washed up on shore, and, in one of their jawbones, was a tooth stump that fitted the fragment that Pennycuick found at the campsite. Back in Dawson City, O'Brian was charged with the murder of the three travellers on the trail and sentenced to hang for his crime. Death was a constant companion in the North, regardless of whether it was by murder or dying from the forces of nature.[8]

Dempster and the men crawled into their tent and settled on spruce branches. They had full stomachs and were tired from the day of mushing and the slipping and sliding on the glacier. There were still kilometres more of glacier ice to climb the next morning. Knowing that they had several days of physically draining work ahead of them, they wanted to get an early start. There was one thing they did not know, however. Despite all the thorough planning, and despite the vast experience of Dempster and his men, and their honorable motive — it would all be in vain. Death had won on the Arctic trail. Fitzgerald, Carter, Taylor, and Kinney were already dead.

FIFTEEN
Ascending the Glaciers

The nameless men who nameless rivers travel,
And in strange valleys great strange deaths alone;
The grim, intrepid ones who would unravel
The mysteries that shroud the Polar Zone.[1]

LEFT CAMP AT 7:45.... TRAIL VERY GOOD. THE BIG GLACIER WAS VERY SLIPPERY, AND WE HAD THE SAME DIFFICULTY AS YESTERDAY.

On March 3, after a breakfast of bannock and tea, Dempster and the men wasted no time in breaking camp, loading the sleds and hitching up the dog teams. Bringing out the axe once more the patrol chopped steps in the ice and laboured their way up the slippery slope. Once more ice was like a sheet of glass. The dogs were pulling and straining, all the while trying to stand upright on four legs. Despite having been carefully scraped the night before, the leather-clad sled runners soon became as icy and slick as the surface they were traversing, creating further difficulty for the panting dogs. Though movement was almost impossible, they somehow managed to find secure enough footing to get them across the Seela Pass. At the rate they were going, they would reach the Blackstone River the following day. They were glad to make it into a stretch of timber where the spindly black spruce grew as close together as porcupine quills before nightfall. At this time they were still on the Twelve Mile River, but decided to make camp at 4:30 p.m.

A raging fire helped take the chill out of the air and the hungry men sat down to eat. Of course, the dogs had been tended to first and the pleas from the excited huskies soon quieted down as dried fish was tossed to each hungry animal. Just as dried fish was the staple food for the dogs, beans were the staple for patrol travel. Since beans take a long time to cook, before any patrol was made a huge pot of the small round pods were soaked overnight to soften, then cooked. Once the beans were tender, they were spread out on a wooden plank that rested between two saw-horses outside the detachment. They would freeze in a thin sheet, almost like peanut brittle. Once frozen, the beans were broken into chunks and stuffed into flour sacks ready for the trail.

Whoever was doing the cooking for the patrol may have tossed some bacon into the pot to boil along with the beans to add some flavour. This patrol would have packed many of the same provisions that Fitzgerald had, but unlike Fitzgerald's patrol, Dempster's had the good fortune of starting in Dawson City where they had access to a greater quantity and a wider selection of food than the Mounties that began from Fort McPherson.

While sitting around the campfire, the men likely discussed where they thought the patrol could have run into trouble. The information brought by Esau George that Fitzgerald and the men were lost a week after leaving Fort McPherson, indicated to Dempster that the patrol had been uncertain of the route. Dempster, who always had a guide with him on patrol, knew that Fitzgerald had let Esau George go after being lost, a decision that just didn't make sense to him. Dempster's investigative mind turned the facts over and over; he was almost certain that the winter patrol had turned around and was safely back in Fort McPherson.

Each day on the trail Dempster and the men were also on the lookout for a sign of any First Nations people in the wilderness who might have word on the Fort McPherson men's whereabouts. So far, Dempster and his men had seen neither, but it was still early on, and they really hadn't expected to find any signs of the missing patrol so soon.

Light clouds were beginning to form overhead, and the tempera-ture was warming up. There was no show of the northern lights. The only sound was that of water running under the icy surface of the Twelve Mile River. It was a peaceful setting and one where Jack Dempster felt he belonged. He had a strong affinity with this environment and loved the trail. He loved the smell of the snow, the smell of the icy riverbeds, the smoke from the campfires, and just about everything around him. He loved the open spaces, the feeling of being a part of something so powerful, and to be engaged in a challenge with the forces of nature. The men who patrolled the Yukon were tough and purposeful. They were resourceful and they respected the knowledge that nature was always in control.[2] They also appreciated the quiet moments of peace that seemed to enter the soul on a night like that of March 3, 1911.

MARCH 4TH. ZERO, LIGHT SNOW FALL ... LEFT CAMP AT 7:30 A.M.

They were off, the sleds seemingly weightless behind the dogs. The going was good, but it wasn't long before the Mounties arrived at their next obstacle; another glacier loomed in front of them. Thankfully, the surface of this one was more stable for climbing. The temperature was cold enough to maintain a freeze, they didn't have to contend with wet moccasins. They were, however, faced with a very steep grade, which caused them considerable

Climbing steep and ice-covered terrain presented continual strain on both dogs and men. The huskies, bred for this type of work, were extreme athletes and willing workers.

difficulty. Since timing was urgent, they worked themselves into a sweat, again hacking steps into the side of the glacier with the axe and hauling the heavily loaded sleds alongside the dogs. Dempster's diary entry was typically understated and focused on the facts, saying only that the patrol had "considerable difficulty in getting up and this was also the case on the two glaciers on the Blackstone, very hard on both men and dogs." The gains they had made initially had been lost over these past two days.

By noon they had made it to a small cabin, where they stopped for a quick lunch, then headed on their way. They were now off the glacier. The day had been a long one, and at 6:15 p.m. they set up their camp. They were about five kilometres above the Blackstone food cache. Dempster noted that there was hardly any snow and that moss and grass were showing up all along the trail. If the temperatures warmed further, the dogs would be faced with pulling the sleds over the burgeoning of spring thaw, hauling over patchy, bare, and slushy snow-covered ground, mushy from the melt.

Technically it was still winter, but signs of overflow, moss, and grass signalled that the patrol could be in for some difficult conditions. It was known that the trail they were on from Dawson City to Fort McPherson was only viable in the winter months. This late patrol was indeed pushing its luck. With no snow to bury boulders and other obstacles, they would now need to manoeuvre even more carefully, which would increase their travel time. If fortune was with them, the snow would once again begin to fall.

The Mounties had put in a very long day, almost twelve hours. They were soon wrapped in sleeping bags inside the shelter of their tent. Strained muscles relaxed, but poor Turner was in agony because of his frostbitten feet. His managing to climb the glaciers with feet in such bad condition gave testament to his dedication to his job.

MARCH 5TH, 10 BELOW, WINDY AND SNOWING.

By morning the early spring had been chased away by winter. The relief patrol, on the trail by 7:40 a.m., was being mercilessly battered by forceful winds and blowing snow. The previous day's spring-like weather was much better than what they were currently battling. The men faced another hill, and once again had to hack out snow steps, then double up the dog teams to get the sleds up the hill. It was one hill climb after the other as they struggled towards their next lunch stop at Christmas Creek.

Hot tea and hot food gave them the fuel needed to carry on, following the contours of Christmas Creek to the next summit. The trail was filled with drifting snow, making passage extremely difficult, and they were happy to set up camp in a treed area again. It was 7:00 p.m., making it almost another twelve-hour day of slogging. Dempster wrote: "Men and dogs very tired to-night; the wind was blowing in a gale down the creek; no dry wood here."

Gathering what they could for firewood, the Mounties coaxed a sputtering flame into a fire that smoldered more than burned. Green wood is most disappointing when it comes to campfires. Although more smoke than heat was being generated, sitting in a smoky campfire and being surrounded by the scraggly spruce was comforting. This was their sixth day on the trail, and, despite the challenges of the glaciers, they had covered a good distance.

Setting up a camp within timber helped to shelter the Mounties from nature's weather shifts. The snowshoes of the First Nations guide were much larger than the standard issue snowshoes the Mounties used.

The tent was set up under the protection of the spruce trees, but snow-flakes continued to fall, and every now and then the accumulation of snow slid off the sloped roof, landing in a thud beside the walls of the tent. This wasn't a bad thing since it created a wind barrier, which helped to keep the warmth inside their shelter. The four tired men were soon sound asleep, resting and restoring hard-worked muscles. The sound of snores competed with the Arctic wind that began to increase in tempo during the night. Soon the tent walls were quivering with the blasts. Nature's fury was beginning to build.

MARCH 6TH. ZERO. STRONG WIND ALL LAST NIGHT AND THIS MORNING.

Even though the temperature was zero, the wind chill made it seem more like -40°C below. As the patrol headed down the big glacier, the going was treacherous. The fact that there were no falls resulting in broken bones was remarkable. That applied to the dogs as well, all of which were trying to keep upright whenever the toboggans were slipping sideways. The men had to walk alongside to keep the sleds straight and prevent their sliding into the harnessed teams.

After coming down the glacier, the patrol was met with further tough going. The portage had been filled in with great drifts of snow, and, with the Arctic air blowing, the surface had become a thick crust, creating very difficult walking conditions. Things became progressively worse and by late afternoon the men encountered overflow water about thirty centimetres deep. The snowshoes had to come off. Not only did their moccasins freeze as they proceeded, but the men were soaked as they sloshed through the icy water. At 4:15 p.m. they quit for the day and set up camp. Changing into dry gear was a welcome relief. The dogs needed special care that night because of having strained muscles from half-walking and half-swimming through shoulder-deep water. Their heavy coats were soaked through to the skin, and the exhausted dogs must have been chilled to the bone.

Once the fire was going and the dogs checked for injury and fed, the tent was set up, wet clothes were hug to dry, and food was tossed into the pot. Their tea, flavoured with smoke from the campfire, was immediately gulped down. Each night was almost the same as the night before. The only differences were weather conditions and their location on the trail.

Dempster's patrol had been out for a week, and the men were feeling the effects of the difficult terrain and wind chill from the Arctic front. Turner was still dealing with his frostbitten feet and although the mere thought of travelling through icy overflow would intimidate most men, he continued to do his share and keep up with the rest as they climbed, slid, and slipped their way to Fort McPherson. It didn't seem to matter from what location the Mounties started from, the winter patrols of 1910–11 were struggling. The official patrol had already failed.

The wind kept up its assault, and, with that, the temperature dropped. Snow was swirling, creating blizzard-like conditions. There would be no signs of grasses or moss when the patrol awoke the next morning.

MARCH 7TH. 15 BELOW. STRONG WIND AND SNOW

Braving the storm, they were off again by 7:45 a.m. Blowing snow found its way inside parka hoods and melted on sweaty necks. Snowshoes crunched through the drifts and the cadence of the dogs' breath became quick and shallow as they pulled the heavy toboggans. Then, just over an hour into their day's travel, they hit water again. Off came the snowshoes, and the next two hours were a chilly wet torture for both men and huskies. The dogs were pulling the sleds through forty-five centimetres of frigid slush as the men ran alongside them, their moccasins throwing up rooster tails of icy granules. At 11:35 a.m., once they hit solid ground again, the patrol stopped to change out of their frozen footwear. They ate some lunch, then proceeded to meet the raging blizzard. In spite of the terrible weather and steep terrain, the patrol managed to cross the divide between Michel Creek and Hart River — no easy task.

A gale blowing from the north sculpted the fallen snow into huge drifts, filling the trail over the divide. Dempster wrote in his log that the going was "very heavy." At 4:35 p.m. the men arrived at a cabin on the Big Hart River and decided to stop for the night. After a week on the trail, sleeping under a roof would be welcome, but just because they didn't have to set up their tent, it didn't mean all the rest of their chores were eliminated. Dogs, firewood, fire, hanging wet gear to dry, cooking food … and on it went.

Back in Dawson City, the superintendent must have been concerned. Fitzgerald's patrol hadn't arrived, Dempster hadn't sent an update with a runner, and there had been no reports from any First Nations with information of either the Dempster patrol or the Fitzgerald patrol. Snyder had nothing to forward to Commissioner Bowen Perry. The waiting continued.

Snyder had confidence in Dempster's abilities, and the Dawson patrol had wisely hired a guide to accompany them, but he knew that the forces of nature always had the upper hand. Fitzgerald was known as the "Northern Man."[3] Knowing Fitzgerald's vast experience and his respect for what nature could send his way, Synder could only wonder as to what could have caused the problem. All he could hope for was that both patrols would end up safely in Fort McPherson, but to find that out one patrol would have to turn around and come back to Dawson to let him know all was fine. Then and only then could he forward the information to the commissioner in Regina.

Given that thirty was the average number of days on the trail for a northern patrol, it would take sixty days for Dempster to make it to Fort McPherson and then back to Dawson to report on his findings. That would mean it would be April before any news was confirmed, unless the Fitzgerald party was found somewhere near Dawson and was brought in by Dempster, or a messenger brought news from the corporal.

MARCH 8TH. 62 BELOW, COLD, CLEAR.

Moving from terrain with green grass showing through the snowmelt, and moss-covered rocks, to a bitterly cold -52°C and piles of fresh snow just proved to the men that nothing was constant in the North except the unexpected. Bundled up in as much clothing as they could to keep warm, they tramped on the fresh snowfall, which Dempster described as "heavy." At this point they were between glaciers, heading through the canyon along Wolf Creek. At some points they completely lost the trail and yet they would manage to find it again and keep on going when, unexpectedly, the going took a nasty turn. Dempster wrote: "On the first glacier above the canyon we got into water about a foot deep, and lost about half an hour." With soaking feet in frozen moccasins, they carried on to the second glacier. At the upper end of it they made camp. It would become dangerous for both men and the dogs if they didn't warm up at the first opportunity.

Mists shrouded the glacier and clung to the open camp that seemed so small and insignificant in the enormity of the landscape. Yet the purpose of the four men trying to absorb some heat from the feeble flames was anything but.

SIXTEEN
The First Clue

But the Yukon service where the Police were at the beck and call of every case of need or distress or danger, no matter how much hardship and exposure they involved, was taking its toll. The men of the corps were paying the price for the proud privilege of preserving the Pax Britannica.[1]

The small settlement back at Fort McPherson assumed all was going well. The winter patrol had left eleven weeks ago. They expected to hear from a return patrol, bringing news and mail, and tales of their patrol's time spent in the "big" city of Dawson. Of course Fitzgerald and the officers would be writing reports, but there would have been time to hear news from the "Outside," as it was called. Mail only came twice a year, so this was an eagerly anticipated event.

The isolated town had been very quiet since December 21, when the RNWMP dogs had been taken for the patrol, except for "Bob." Bob had come from Herschel Island with Fitzgerald and been injured along the way and was given the chance to heal at McPherson. The RNWMP dogs always created a ruckus when anyone was outside with them, and were considered pets and treated like members of the community when not working.

The inhabitants at Fort McPherson had no idea that the Mounties had not arrived in Dawson City, nor did they know that a relief patrol had been sent to look for them. Likewise they had no way of knowing that Fitzgerald, Taylor, Kinney, and Carter had become lost, run out of food, and turned around to come home, and finally had perished along the trail. No news was good news for settlers in Fort McPherson, and they continued to look out for, and expect, the patrol to return each day.

MARCH 9TH. 50 BELOW, COLD, THICK FOG AND GLACIER.

Dempster and the men got a later start than usual, but by 8:00 a.m. they were on the glacier. An hour into the climb, the Mounties had made it to the upper canyon portage, but found the trail had been completely filled in and was again "very heavy." They found the route had flooded, and spent a great deal of time taking a detour to avoid the water, all the while faltering in a suffocating fog. Once they located another route, they met with further difficulties — the divide from Wolf to Forrest creek was also completely filled in with overflow. However, this was the end of the first leg of their route, and at 5:20 p.m., about two miles from Forrest Creek, they set up camp.

Glenbow Archives, PD-383-2-17.

The tall black spruce averages five to fifteen metres in height. These ice-pruned asymmetrical trees often tilt at an alarming angle and are referred to as "drunken trees." The lean is associated with the freezing and thawing of the permafrost in which these far northern trees grow.

The dogs were beyond exhausted, wet, and in need of attention. If they became too fatigued at this point in the patrol they would never make it to Fort McPherson, and without the dogs the men would be in deep trouble. There were still hundreds of kilometres to go.

Considering the weather and the deplorable conditions of the terrain the men were following, would they have a chance of locating any sign of the lost patrol? Snow, water, and wind were all playing a role in obliterating any visible signs of others having been in the vicinity. Not only were conditions hindering the search, but frostbite had already claimed Tuner's feet, and with the temperatures at well below -55°C, the rest of the patrol were also at risk of frostbite and hyperthermia.

Dempster knew the importance of stopping to eat and to fuel their bodies. If they didn't, the patrol would not have the inner reserves to battle the harsh weather and ward off the life-threatening symptoms caused by exposure. While shelter, food, and warmth were essential for survival, other factors were required. One also needed to be acutely aware of when to stop and rest. In the North, the hero is not always the one who never gives up, but the one with the wisdom to save one's strength for another day or for when conditions improve, and thus increase the chances of survival.

Once the fire was going, the drained men relaxed around the warmth generated from the flames. It would not be a late night. Drowsy from the heat, they headed into the tent.

MARCH 10TH. 15 BELOW.

By 7:45 a.m. the Mounties were breaking trail. Battling their way through great quantities of newly fallen snow, both the plodding men on snowshoes and the struggling huskies were sinking into the waist-high depths. They strained with each step, scrutinizing the frigid landscape for any indication that Fitzgerald and his patrol had passed this way. The search party was now heading down Forrest Creek, and had Inspector Fitzgerald and his patrol been on the correct route, there should have been a sign here for the searchers to find, but there was nothing. There was nothing for Dempster's men to observe, despite their continued vigilance.

Their clothes were soaked with sweat from the physical exertion. In the brutally cold temperature the garments began to freeze, but this did not seem to faze them and they kept up a good pace. By 2:15 p.m. they had reached the Little Wind River, where another portage had to be crossed. Staggering through the Yukon wilderness and breaking trail as they went, the men finally made it to their next stop. Dempster wrote: "This is the last camping place for some distance." At 4:45 p.m. the Mounties began the set up for the night.

Checking the dogs required the undivided attention of all men, since the last few days had been very difficult for the canines. This was day eleven on the Dempster patrol, and although the dogs had not had to pull heavy loads all that time, the fluctuating temperatures had taken an extra toll since they could not habituate to a single temperature range. The colder the temperatures were, the more food they required to maintain heat and energy than on warmer days. Fortunately, there was plenty of dried fish for food, and the sleds could be dug into the snow and set up as a windbreak to help buffer the Arctic winds. As always, the men paid scrupulous attention to the dogs' needs. Once noses buried themselves under tails, the men could tend to their own nightly jobs and prepare their own meal.

As the night progressed, the wind began to increase in force, whipping the flickering flames. Soon the wind became a gale, blowing the flames sideways and scattering ash across the camp. The wind blew along the surface of the Little Wind River, carrying with it the icy chill. A constant companion of the northern regions, the Inuit had an important legend honouring the wind. One story tells of how it can cause death to those who do not treat others with respect.

———◆———

An orphan boy living in an Arctic village was badly mistreated by those in his community. Cruel neighbors would taunt him and pull at his clothes and rip them. His grandmother made him new clothing from the skins of caribou, but this did not stop these bullies from coming to the boy's house and once again ripping his new clothes. His grandmother became very frustrated and one day she took the young boy down to the sea and threw him into the water. She called to him and said, "You will surface on the water as a *natsiavinaapik*, a seal pup."

Just as his grandmother had promised, the boy turned into a seal pup and swam happily in the sea. His grandmother said, "When the hunters chase you, lead them far from shore, then spread your arms when you reach the water's surface and *Ungallak!*" — the noise a seal makes with its flippers.

Very soon, some of the men who had mistreated the boy saw the seal pup and decided to hunt it. They threw their harpoons at the seal, but they failed time and again. There were many hunters after the seal pup, but none were able to kill him. The seal pup did as his grandmother said, and he led the hunters far, far away from shore. Then he surfaced, and clapped his flippers as fast as he could. This caused a big wind and raging seas, and the hunters, in their *qajait*, the small watercraft, were caught in the storm waves caused by the wind made from the seal's flippers. They were unable to reach the safety of land, and all drowned.

In this way, the Inuit children were taught never to mistreat any human being. Instead, they learned to make peace with others and develop more positive attitudes.[2] The harsh gales were a constant reminder of the need to respect and treat others with kindness.

MARCH 11. 35 BELOW, STRONG WIND, FOGGY.

By morning the wind was no less ferocious and the men set off into the frenzy of yet another storm. It was an early start at 7:40 a.m. The fog rolled in as they were making their way along the river. Into the afternoon they encountered water running over the icy surface, somewhat frozen but not solid enough to carry the sleds. The curved front of the toboggans broke through the fragile ice and sprayed the frozen overflow. This slushy mess created torture for the huskies' paws. Time was lost as the men tried to find a way around the water, but, failing to do so, they continued to slosh their way forward. The gale was a constant companion and the cold cut to their very bones.

Sore and bruised feet, frostbite, frozen eyelashes, teeth aching from cold air, and laboured breathing, were all a part of the daily job. Also part of the job was the search. Nothing had turned up on day twelve that they could see. The absence of any trace of Fitzgerald's patrol suggested that the winter patrol had turned around and headed back to Fort McPherson, but then the question remained: Why?

After braving the bitter temperatures for nine hours, the patrol made camp. A temperature of -37°C with a strong wind would make it feel more like -95°C and there was the real danger of exposure unless the men stopped to drink something hot and light a fire. Dempster had the best interest of his men and dogs in mind when he called it quits for the day.

The weather was a constant concern. The black sky was clear and stars were gradually emerging.

———————◆———————

To the Inuit, the stars were once living beings. The stars were not just put into the night sky to give light or to guide the traveller, they were the living, sent by some twist of fate, to roam the heavens, never swerving. One living creature who went to live in the sky was Nanuk, the bear.

Nanuk was out hunting for food. He met a fierce pack of Inuit hunting dogs. The dogs began to attack Nanuk. Terrified, the hapless bear started to run. He ran and he ran, with the savage dogs chasing him. Neither seemed to tire. They ran over the ice, the bear in the lead with the dogs right behind him. Nanuk could not shake the dogs, no matter how hard he tried. The chase went on for a very long time, right to the edge of the earth, but neither bear nor dogs noticed, as they were too caught up in the chase.

When they reached the edge of the earth they plunged over into the sky, turning into stars as they went. The stars are permanent in position and the constellation is called the Great Bear.[3]

Of the dogs that pursued him, nothing is known.

———————◆———————

The Mounties stacked more chopped wood onto the fire to help keep what warmth they could around the dogs, then crawled wearily into the tent for some well-deserved sleep. Perhaps the clear night sky, with Great

Bear shining in full view was a sign that the chase was coming to an end. Maybe the patrol would find some answers the next day.

MARCH 12TH, 42 BELOW, COLD, FOGGY.

At 7:40 a.m., the patrol headed out into the sharp Arctic air. The dogs hauled the sleds alongside the river. Dempster wrote that the dogs were: "pulling over [sand] bars part of [the] time and part of [the time was] good going." Then they saw it. On day thirteen the Mounties struck an old trail at about 9:30 a.m. and surmised that they could now be on the Fitzgerald's trail.

As they followed it, Dempster mulled the possibilities over in his mind. Could this be the police trail? Or it could be a trail made by a First Nations group? All they had at this point was a difficult-to-follow flooded-over trail. There was no evidence of whose trail, and it wasn't even an obvious trail, but it was clear enough for the keen eyes of one who had travelled these routes on several occasions. Even though it was partially erased by water, every so often they could pick up the signs, especially on the sand bars towards the mouth of the river. This could be very good news, as it would imply that the patrol had turned around and returned to Fort McPherson. If all had gone well, they would be back by now. But if that was the case, what caused them to make this decision?

In any event, this was what the patrol was looking for — a sign of life. They now had something to follow and to gather their evidence from as they went along.

By 2:05 p.m. Dempster and the men had made it to the Big Wind River, and there the men divided up and went searching in different directions for signs of the winter patrol. Stewart, the First Nations guide, and Dempster went up the Big Wind River for "some distance," as Dempster put it, crossing and re-crossing the river from bank to bank trying to find something, anything, that would lead the relief patrol in the direction of the trail they had found. Dempster and Stewart had no success, so they came back and met up with Fyfe and Turner. They too had not had any success and so all four then headed down river. As they proceeded down they picked up the trail, only to lose it again. At 4:45 p.m. they decided to stop for the day, and the men crossed the river to set up camp under the black spruce. Ironically, it was here that they found what they had been searching for — an overnight camp of Fitzgerald, Carter, Kinney, and Taylor.

Had there been a First Nations camp in the area, Dempster might have hired a runner to take word back to Superintendent Snyder and let him know that the relief patrol had found an overnight camp of Fitzgerald's winter patrol, and that the logical conclusion would be that Fitzgerald's patrol had for some reason run into trouble and returned to Fort McPherson. However, there was no First Nations group to be found. The superintendent would be kept waiting until there was an opportunity to send word.

Camping in the same camp that had first been set up by Fitzgerald must have been strange. There were signs a tree had been chopped for firewood, and stumps for seats circled a charred fire pit. It would make sense to just use the same fire pit, sit on the same logs cut for seats and chain the dogs to the same trees. If only there were some signs as to why the patrol had turned back, something that would give a real clue as to the whereabouts of the Fort McPherson men.

There were no voices to speak as to why. The only sounds were the cracking fire, the water running under the ice, and the air that moved through the scraggly stand of timber.

SEVENTEEN
Following the Trail

It's the fingers that freeze
In the boreal breeze —
It's the COLD,
COLD,
COLD[1]

MARCH 13. 45 BELOW, CLEAR, THICK FOG OVER OPEN WATER.

Dempster and the men got an early start. By 7:40 a.m. they were following what they believed to be the trail from the inspector's patrol. This was what the search patrol had been looking for, and after two weeks they finally had signs to follow, but it would by no means be an easy job. Just when the old trail was found, it would vanish again in the snow pack. What was causing the most puzzlement, however, was the fact that the trail Fitzgerald's patrol made was not the common route. Dempster wrote that the trail "went around the river instead of going over [the] portage."

Travel was hard going. Much of the trail they were following was crusted snow, which was hard on the dog's paws. Once they encountered thick fog, the speed at which they had been going slowed dramatically. The dense air made it difficult to determine their direction and obstacles were a challenge to spot.

Six kilometres into the day they came across a second night camp, also thought to be that of Fitzgerald and his men. There, the Mounties found a butter tin, a corned beef tin, and a piece of flour sack marked "R.N.W.M. Police, Fort McPherson." The fact that the camps were so close together could well have raised questions for Dempster. Had the patrol become lost and spent the day looking for the route, and in using precious daylight, then been forced to set up a camp close to the one from the previous night? Or had they just been lost in the fog and decided to not venture far?

Being as watchful as possible in the near whiteout conditions, the relief patrol followed the parts of the old trail until 5:30 p.m. When they reached a point about eleven kilometres below Mount Deception, the patrol stopped for the night. Now that the "Iron Man of the Trail" had found what he was searching for, it must have been tough to call it quits for the day. All signs were pointing to the Fitzgerald patrol having returned to Fort McPherson, so the faster the relief could go, the sooner they would have their answers and be able to turn around and head back to Dawson City to inform the superintendent. But Dempster's innate sense of caution held sway — something wasn't quite right.

It was a cold and bitter night, even though spring was officially only a few days away. The dogs had had a very tough day and were settled in a heap after being checked and fed. Once more the men enacted the mundane routine of camp set up and cooking and were once again sitting around the campfire. It was just another night in the North for the members of the patrol. Discussion likely would have included speculation about what had gone wrong with the inspector's winter patrol. An officer would always be running scenarios though his head. Why? Where? Where? When? In this case, it was mostly why.

During the night the snow began to fall and the flakes settled like a blanket over the dogs. It is odd that the very elements that create cold and frostbite are the same that can be used to provide shelter and trap warmth. Snug under the layer of whiteness the huskies lay sleeping.

MARCH 14TH. 30 BELOW, CLOUDY, LIGHT SNOW.

By 7:45 a.m., the lightly falling snow found its way into every nook and cranny of the men's kits and food bags before the loaded sleds were covered.

After harnessing the huskies and strapping on snowshoes, the men called to the dogs. The teams pulled in their traces and they were off. Dempster wrote that the travelling was good for the most part, although parts of the trail were filled in and heavy going. For thirty kilometres beside the Big Wind River they picked up Fitzgerald's old trail a few times, but repeatedly lost it again. Dempster wrote that the men also located and passed by a cluster of three more of Fitzgerald's night camps, none of which were more than "five miles apart."

The men mushed forward to Mount Deception and prepared for the climb over the portage. The sky was heavy with clouds and there was an oppressiveness about the place. Snow crusted the surface of the trail and threatened to shred the tender pads on the dogs' paws. To help lessen the chance of damage, the patrol slowed their pace. The dogs were their lifeline. Both canines and the Mounties continued with purpose.

At the campfire that night Dempster thought about the trail and the winter patrol. His thinking was that because the camps were so close together, the inspector and men had turned around and headed north. When would they have done that? And the more significant question, the one to which he kept returning, why? It had taken Dempster and his relief patrol thirteen days to reach the first sign of Fitzgerald and the winter patrol. That would then indicate that the winter patrol was two-thirds of their way to Dawson, or roughly eighteen days into their patrol, using the average thirty-day patrol time. If the Inspector turned around after eighteen days, and had a return of eighteen days, then the winter patrol should have reached Fort McPherson by January 25, or thereabouts, and that was over six weeks ago — unless something had gone terribly wrong. Again, Dempster puzzled over Fitzgerald's decision to dispense with Esau George as a guide.

Dempster's own guide, Special Constable Stewart, grew up in a tribe who lived in accordance with traditions. Their lives were organized around the rhythms of nature. If they were near the Arctic Ocean, the level of the tide or state of the ice dictated how their day would be spent. The weather conditions made them focus on things like shelter and where to camp. Day to day life was linked to the elements of their environment. Their land was their strength, they believed, but could also be the reason for sorrow.

Dempster's views had been greatly influenced by his good relationship with the First Nations people. Having learned much about the northern regions from them, he was also attuned to his surroundings. He recognized the importance of understanding that in a challenge with the forces of nature, nature will win.

The tent was cold, but the spruce boughs scented the air and provided a sense of comfort inside the canvas. The nights always seemed to be short, and before they knew it the relief patrol was up and stuffing sleeping blankets into kit bags and rummaging around for dry socks and woollen shirts.

MARCH 15TH. 15 BELOW, CLEAR IN A.M., CLOUDY AND WARM IN P.M.

At 7:25 a.m. the teams were struggling on the trail. Later that morning the patrol arrived at Waugh's tent and found that Inspector Fitzgerald and the men had spent the night there as well. With this confirmation that they were on the right trail, the men headed off again. The snow was wet and heavy and the dogs tired early from hauling the sleds, but stoutly continued to pull. The men were continually looking for signs of Fitzgerald's trail, and every now and then, as before, they would spot parts. When they arrived at the mouth at the Big Wind River, where the river surface was solid, they saw them — the imprint of snowshoe tracks. For a distance of about a hundred metres the snow was blown off the surface, leaving the old trail hard and standing high off the ice of the river. The tracks were heading down the Big Wind. This was another clue that confirmed Dempster's idea that Fitzgerald and the winter patrol had turned around. It was tempting to hurry down the contours of the Big Wind, but the dogs' paws were still a concern and safety came first.

Following the snowshoe tracks, they carried on down the river's edge where Dempster saw further evidence that the trail Fitzgerald had made had taken them to the mouth of Mountain Creek and up the creek instead of crossing the intended portage. This deviation would have added an additional five kilometres to the winter patrol's journey. The men continued to follow Fitzgerald's trail and stopped at 5:20 p.m., after having travelled just over six kilometres up Mountain Creek.

Conversation around the campfire would almost certainly have been focused on the evidence the patrol found that day. First they found a camp, then three more in close proximity to each other, followed by snowshoe tracks heading back towards Fort McPherson. Unfortunately, Dempster and the men had still not encountered a First Nations group, so were unable to send this news back to Dawson City. Superintendent Snyder must also have been wondering what was happening, but until word came in all he could do was wait. At this same time at Fort McPherson, the tiny community must have wondered why their patrol and dog teams hadn't come back. They had been gone for almost three months.

The temperature was increasing and with that change any snow that had balanced on bare tree limbs or spruce needles plopped to the ground. The running water from Mountain Creek began to gurgle louder. The night air was filled with soft sounds. Perhaps the men had a good feeling about the day, encouraged by the strong hunch that the Fitzgerald winter patrol had arrived safely back in Fort McPherson.

MARCH 16TH. ZERO, CLOUDY.

Heading up Mountain Creek at 7:45 a.m., the men found the trail very heavy going and once again the men had to assist the dogs in hauling the toboggans. The weather was continuing to warm and their moccasins soaked up moisture from the melting snow. Just over an hour later, they came across a cabin where Dempster and the men made a gruesome discovery. Dempster wrote: "I found cached a toboggan, wrapper and seven sets of dog harnesses which I have no doubt were cached here by Fitzgerald's party on their return trip to McPherson. In cabin also we found the paws of a dog cut off at the knee joint, also a shoulder blade which had been cooked and the flesh evidently eaten."

Their hearts must have sunk. Nothing could have prepared them for what they found. Frozen dog paws and dog bones? For the inspector and his men to resort to eating their dogs they must have been in serious trouble. And seven harnesses? At this point Dempster must have wondered if the men would have had sufficient dogs to take them back to Fort McPherson. Four men, two sleds, and only eight dogs and hundreds of kilometres left to go? Although the situation did not look good, Dempster wrote: "I felt confident that the party had returned to McPherson in safety." There was no further evidence in or around the cabin to give any other ideas as to what had happened.

Since there were still many hours left in the day, the relief party headed off again, following the snowshoe prints further up Mountain Creek. At 4:00 p.m., with their dogs on the brink of refusing to on, the men stopped at the foot of the "Big Hill." They didn't have the heart to try and push their huskies any further. Dempster left Turner, Fyfe, and Stewart to tend to them and set up camp, and he headed up the hill to break a trail for the next morning. All the way up the creek, he found the trail filled with drifted snow. The work was exhausting, but Dempster wanted to make things easier for the dogs the following morning. He was also on the look-out for any further signs of the winter patrol.

After tamping down the heavy snowdrifts and setting the trail for the next day, he returned to camp. Unease filled the relief patrol this night, and even though the temperature was warming up rapidly, the air held a certain chill. Thoughts might have centred on Fitzgerald and the desperation that prompted his men to have killed and eaten seven dogs. When were they at the cabin on Mountain Creek? How long had the winter patrol been in trouble? Did they make it back to Fort McPherson? The thought of finding their fellow officers dead was unthinkable but now seemed a possibility. And yet the RNWMP had never had a multiple loss of members. Surely they must have made it back.

Dempster wrote: "Although everything along the Big Wind river seemed to indicate that the party had returned to McPherson, this discovery was the first positive proof that they had turned back, and also that they were short of provisions...."

Maybe sleep did not come easy to the tired men. Maybe they each had memories of Kenny, Taylor, Carter, and Fitzgerald. RNWMP officers were like family to each other. Maybe they couldn't bear to think of the possible outcome and instead slipped into slumber. Either way, the following morning they would be on the search again and likely with even more urgency.

In that very cabin, exactly forty-six days earlier, Fitzgerald and his exhausted men had taken refuge. Tired eyes, showing no flicker of interest, had stared at each other reflecting their emptiness. They had slept for the night and arisen the next morning to continue their way back to Fort McPherson, just as the relief patrol led by Dempster would be doing.

MARCH 17TH. 5 ABOVE, CLOUDY, WINDY ON HILL.

Even though Dempster had blazed the trail the night before, with the warm temperature and the physical exertion of climbing the Big Hill, the men were soaked in sweat and the dogs were heavily panting by the time they reached the top. By 9:00 a.m. they were at the top of the first hill. Keeping hydrated after such exertion was important, especially since the temperature had rising so drastically in the past week. The wind did help to keep the dogs somewhat cool, but the wind also would have frozen the Mounties' sweat-soaked clothing.

The relief patrol was able to follow Fitzgerald's return trail but with much difficulty. The snow was a white soggy blanket, and the dogs were tiring as they pulled the sleds. The patrol stopped to camp, five kilometres up the north fork of the Caribou Born River. It was 5:20 p.m. They had put in ten hours of tough going, and the area was new to Dempster and the men. By now they were following a trail that was well off the normal patrol routes previously taken, and this route, although it did not go over the mountain, was much longer than the usual Dawson-Fort McPherson trail. Fitzgerald had added many more kilometres to his return journey, and this had cost him more days travelling. Why the winter patrol had struck this trail was a mystery to Dempster.

The tired dogs and tired men ate. Then the dogs curled into furry balls in the snow, allowing sleep to come. The patrol had been searching for almost three weeks and not only had the dogs been pushing hard, but they also had to withstand the abrasive surface of the crusty snow. It wasn't just Turner who had sore feet!

Dempster had made little "booties" for the dogs to help safeguard against possible injury, but his lead dog kept losing his, causing more work for Dempster as he would then have to make another pair. This was cause for some irritation, but the devoted Mountie did not want a lame dog in his team, so precaution was better than taking the easy way out and ignoring the problem. A few days later the patrol discovered where all the missing booties had gone. Dempster's wheel dog (the one closest to the sled) had been slow and sluggish for a day or so, and was finally sick. Up came all the booties that the lead dog had "lost."[2]

The men stared into the smoke and the flames of the campfire. The sky above them was filled with clouds and the temperature continued to rise. After experiencing such extremes as -80°C, to have the mercury climb over 70°C to -11°C, must have felt like they were in the tropics. Cloud cover in the North can make the country seem smaller and less majestic and less unforgiving. It didn't seem like such a desolate place that needed to be met in a head-on challenge, yet that is exactly what the Mounties were doing. Meeting the North in all its command — head-on.

MARCH 18TH. 12 ABOVE, CLOUDY.

At 7:40 a.m. the patrol had packed up their camp and harnessed the dogs. They were heading north-northwest up the Caribou River, which would lead them over the divide. Again, this was new territory for them and they had difficulty finding the trail in the dense spruce trees. Dempster wrote that they travelled up and down hills all day, which was exhausting for both men and dogs. By 5:45 p.m. they reached the Trail River, and followed the icy surface, finally finding a place to set up camp at 6:30 p.m.

Nature decided once again to show who was in control. The temperatures started to drop, and, with that, snow began to fall.

EIGHTEEN
The Lost Patrol

My voyaging is nigh its close,
And dark is drifting down.
With weary feet my way I beat ...
So let me take without heart-break
The Trail of No Return.[1]

MARCH 19TH. 15 BELOW, CLOUDY; SNOWING ALL AFTERNOON

Dempster and his men were back on the trail at 7:40 a.m., heading into the whiteness. It was a miserable day to travel, but nonetheless the patrol kept on their search for ten long hours. With the ever-disappearing trail heavy with wet snow, trying to stay on the path made by Fitzgerald over six weeks earlier was a nightmare. Sometimes Dempster wasn't sure they were headed in the right direction, and, at other times, when the relief nearly turned around, a part of the old trail would present itself, only to vanish again, the route blurred by the blowing flakes. The snow fell between the spruce trees, rapidly covering the trail made by the men. Who would be sent out to find them if they too became lost?

At 5:15 p.m., about eight kilometres from the Peel River and in the homestretch to McPherson, they set up their camp and once more sat around the fire. The dim light gave the men's faces a ghostly, disembodied look, resembling spirit ghosts from First Nations' legends — the ghosts of people the North had claimed as her own who were said to come back to haunt familiar settings like this comforting warm place. When more wood was added to the fire, a blaze of smoky light grew and the "ghosts" disappeared, leaving the drained men of the patrol in their places. The chilly ache consuming their bodies gradually lessened as the heat from the flames grew and pipes were lit. It had been a hard day.

Lapsing into silence, Dempster probably looked over his diary, reading to see if there was anything in his words that would hold the clues to the reason why Fitzgerald headed back to Fort McPherson. Why would the winter patrol have taken such a long route? This was perplexing, given that they were so short of food. At the rate the relief patrol was going, they estimated they would be in Fort McPherson within three days, and then, Dempster's questions would be answered. He would, however, find his answers before the three days were up.

MARCH 20TH. 13 BELOW, CLEAR.

Like clockwork, the Mounties were on the trail at 7:40 a.m. To be ready and travelling by this time each morning, they must have been up for more than an hour earlier to have had the time to dismantle their camp, feed themselves and their dogs, and get the teams harnessed and ready for the day. Once again the trail they followed was heavy with wet snow and they struggled to continue their search.

They were on the final stretch into Fort McPherson with about one hundred kilometres left to go. Maintaining their average of thirty kilometres each day would get them into Fort McPherson on the night of the 22nd. Each step took them closer to a warm shelter, company, and meals that didn't consist only of beans, bacon, corned beef in a can, and bannock. The thought helped them keep a good pace through the difficult terrain.

As the sky began to darken, Dempster and the men were approaching Colin Vitisik's cabin. There was no sign of a trail leading to it, but deciding this would be a good place to break their journey, the patrol pulled up the high bank and began to unload their gear. It would be a welcome change to be sleeping inside a log cabin rather than the cold and damp tent that smelled of musty canvas.

Dempster went inside with an armload of gear. As he was hanging his clothing up to dry, he noticed that some packages had been placed on top of a beam. He asked Stewart about them. "I wonder what old Colin has cached up there?" The guide reached up and hauled the heavy bundles off the beam, handing them over to Dempster. They were the dispatch bag marked RNWMP and a bag of mail that had been given to Fitzgerald's patrol the day they left for Dawson City.

Dempster recorded in his diary that he suspected Fitzgerald must have cached the bags to lighten his load, but wondered why the men hadn't come back to retrieve them. The thought of tragedy was kept at bay: "even with this discovery I did not think that any untoward accident had occurred to the party…." He was certain that within a couple of days he would discover why the men hadn't come back to pick up the bags. Dempster also noticed that there was a pile of dog bones by one wall.

The men set to cooking a meal and bringing spruce branches in for their beds. Colin's cabin had been the overnight stop for Fitzgerald before Christmas and then again in early February during his desperate race against time.

Soon pipe smoke was wafting around the rafters and the spruce boughs were scenting the cabin. The men lay down, stretching their tired and muscle-strained legs. In two more days — and easy days at that — they would be settled in real beds, having consumed a home-cooked meal complete with vegetables and fresh buns and maybe even dessert. Then they would catch up on why Fitzgerald and the men had made the decision to turn around and head back to Fort McPherson, hear about the "goings on" from the northern Arctic post at Herschel Island, and visit with the residents they seldom got to see. The thought must have made for a pleasant, quiet evening.

None of them had any idea or were prepared for what they would encounter the following day. The cold that had chilled them to the bone during their journey would not compare to the emotional chill they would feel in just a few short hours.

MARCH 21ST. 13 BELOW, CLOUDY A.M., CLEAR IN P.M.

This would be a day the relief patrol would never forget and a day that would be reported in the world's newspapers.

At 10:00 a.m., after having travelled about fifteen kilometres from Colin's cabin, they reached the Seven Mile Portage and found the tent, tent poles, a plate, and the winter patrol's stove, as well as their thermometer — all alongside the trail. Dempster must have been truly alarmed. He was all too aware that the winter patrol could not have made Fort McPherson from this point in one day with so few dogs left in their teams. So why were their tent, poles, and stove left behind? The patrol urged the dogs into a run. After crossing the Seven Mile Portage, they reached the Peel River again by 2:15 p.m. Forty-five minutes later the patrol was dismayed to find a second toboggan and two sets of dog harnesses lying out on the ice, roughly thirty kilometres from Colin's cabin. Had the winter patrol spent a night out in the open?

The new findings would also mean the patrol was down to one toboggan and six dogs, assuming Dempster and his men had not missed finding other dog harnesses. Dempster noticed the lashings from the runners of the toboggan had been removed. The evidence was pointing to something catastrophic having happened to Fitzgerald, Kinney, Taylor, and Carter.

Taking a careful look around the area, Dempster spotted a trail marked by a simple blue kerchief tied to a willow on the left bank of the river. It led into the bush. What they found at the end of the trail made their hearts sink. Two men from the winter patrol lay dead. Twenty-seven-year-old Constable George Kinney, the three-year veteran of the RNWMP, lay near a spot where once a fire had burned. Drawn and sunken features told of a slow death. He lay on his back, a stiff, frozen bundle of ragged and singed clothing. He was facing upwards, staring at the Yukon sky with sightless eyes.

The sight next to Kinney was even more horrific. Constable Richard O'Hara Taylor, the twenty-eight-year-old officer, a six-year veteran of the RNWMP, lay slumped over the .30-30 carbine rifle. We will never know if there were any strange mutterings reflective of a mind deranged by the ordeal he had suffered, prompted by the realization that his partner on the trail had changed places with death, and that he, Taylor, was now alone.

What is known is that he leaned his head against the rifle, pulled the trigger, and with that, escaped the torture he had endured in the winter wilderness of the Yukon. The shot from the rifle rang out and his face was no longer that of a man. Taylor was found with the gun still grasped in his left hand. Death was his only form of escape.

As the relief patrol moved around the camp, more desperate sights met their eyes. A camp kettle used for cooking held the scraps of the moose-hide lashing on the sleds that had apparently been boiled for any nourishment it could offer. The tea kettle had a bullet hole through it, the one that had killed Taylor.

Dempster and his men cut branches from the willows that surrounded the little open camp and covered the bodies of their friends. It must have been difficult to call to the dogs and leave the bodies of Taylor and Kinney behind, but Fort McPherson was just a day's travel away and the relief patrol would need some assistance. From Dempster's perspective, finding the two men likely meant that Fitzgerald and Carter had left Taylor and Kinney and gone on to get help. But, if the two senior members had made it to Fort McPherson, why hadn't they returned for the two young constables? The unfolding situation was looking grimmer by the minute, but by this time darkness was falling and the relief patrol headed down river to find a camp site.

The evening conversation would have been discussions about Fitzgerald and Carter and their presumably having headed off to get help for the other two. Where were they? Could they still be alive, lost somewhere? By March 21 it was now ninety days since Fitzgerald and the men had mushed away from Fort McPherson. Intuitively, Dempster and his men knew that the likelihood of them being alive was slim.

It must have been a restless night for them, wanting to get on the trail to find any clues and get to Fort McPherson to let people know what they had discovered. Then there would be the trip back to Dawson to inform the superintendent, who would notify the commissioner.

MARCH 22ND. 23 BELOW, CLOUDY, COLD, RAW WIND FROM NOR'WEST.

The harshness of the weather seemed a fitting backdrop to the additional discoveries that Dempster and the men were about to make. They were on the move at 7:25 a.m., but there was no distinct sign of a trail left by Fitzgerald and Carter. For fifteen kilometres along the Peel River, the men searched for clues. Finally, they found snowshoes. More searching turned up a very faint trail leading up the riverbank. Almost hidden within the adjacent bushes lay the bodies of Special Constable Sam Carter and Inspector J.F. Fitzgerald, both dead, lying side by side. They had made it to within forty kilometres of Fort McPherson — a day's travel in normal circumstances.

Carter had died before Fitzgerald. And as a last act to give his partner some dignity, Fitzgerald had dragged Carter's body away from the fire and folded his arms across his chest. His hollowed sunken eyes dominating his gaunt face were then covered with a ragged handkerchief. Fitzgerald was found lying where the fire had once burned, his body frozen into the contours of the ground. His right arm was extended and his left hand was on his chest. The two veterans lay there, their bodies no longer icy cold with the sweat of exhaustion but with the permanence of death.

The four members of the winter patrol of 1910 would now become legends in the Arctic. Maybe the Aurora spirits had called to them, and, in their final stages of starvation and defeat, they walked together along the path, lit by the torches of those who had gone before.

Dempster and the others gathered brush and covered the bodies of Carter and the inspector, then made their way as fast as the dogs could run, reaching Fort McPherson that evening. Breaking the news to the anxious community was a devastating ordeal and the information took some time to register. The town grieved together for the loss of the officers that served them, and especially Lena Oonalina who would have to care for Fitzgerald's daughter on her own. Never in the history of the force had there been such a loss. And this wouldn't be the last. On June 7, 1958, five on duty officers drowned in Lake Simcoe, Ontario while on patrol. Four officers died in a plane crash in Carmacks, Yukon Territories, on July 15, 1963, and on March 3, 2005, almost one hundred years after the deaths of the Lost Patrol, four officers were gunned down at Mayerthorpe, small town outside Edmonton in the line of duty.

There was much to be done. The bodies had to be brought to Fort McPherson, coffins made from wood scrounged from somewhere, and a service held to honour the officers who had paid the ultimate price. Then Dempster and his men would have to make the return journey to Dawson City to relay the devastating incidents a second time. Once in Dawson City, Dempster would also be making a full report of the discoveries and his conclusions regarding the tragic events. There would be an inquiry and interviews and reports from others. The Royal Northwest Mounted Police had never faced such tragedy and the ensuing follow up.

Death does not just end in sorrow.

NINETEEN
The Little Crimson Manual

A constable's life is not altogether an enviable one. He is liable to be exposed to the inclemencies of the weather at all seasons of the year, and is at times called upon to risk his life in the performance of his duty.[1]

Corporal J. Somers and Constable Blake, the RNWMP officers left behind at Fort McPherson, began preparations to return to the scene of the tragedy. Since all the RNWMP dogs were dead, with the exception of Bob, the officers requested the use of the dog teams of Reverend C.E. Whittaker, First Nations guide Peter Ross, and John Firth of the Hudson's Bay Company.[2] The officers also had to borrow sleds to bring back the remains. It would be a heart-wrenching job for those who went on the recovery mission. Blake was left in charge at Fort McPherson.

At 2:00 p.m. on March 23, Corporal Somers, accompanied by Special Constable Jimmie Husky and the First Nations guide Peter Ross, set out upriver with three sleds and the dog teams they had managed to put together. The RNWMP hired special constables from the First Nations community to support the regular members, and although these men did not have the training from Depot, Regina, they were paid full time by the force and could assist in legal matters, arrests, and manage the dog teams. To give them the authority to carry a gun, they were made

"Special Constables" or "Specials." Jimmie Husky was the special constable at Fort McPherson.

The three men made good time and Somers decided to camp thirty kilometres from the fort so that he would be able to get an early start on the 24th, leaving enough time for Peter Ross to retrieve the remains of Fitzgerald and Carter and head back to Fort McPherson that same day. They set up camp just as Dempster and his men and Fitzgerald and his men had done and settled in for the night.

Having left their camp just after dawn on March 24th, the three-man recovery team arrived at 9:30 a.m. at the spot where Inspector Fitzgerald and Constable Carter lay. Once the area had been searched for evidence, they would load Ross's sled with the corpses and he would head back to Fort McPherson while Somers and Husky proceeded to the location of Kinney and Taylor. Somers calculated that Fitzgerald and Carter had made it to within just over forty kilometres of Fort McPherson. Had the winter patrol been healthy and with a five-dog team, they could have made it to Fort McPherson in one day. What a difference a day made!

Concentrating on the job they were there to do, the men got on with their task. Dempster had given directions that the bodies lay within the forest area on the "right limit," at the top of the Peel riverbank. They found the bodies, each covered by half a blanket, and lying under the freshly cut brush that Dempster had placed on them. The two men lay about three metres from each other.

There had been no effort to build a camp at this isolated place. Fitzgerald and Carter, who had devoted their lives to the force that would make Canada a nation unlike any other in the world, had no comforting warmth of a shelter to ward off the frigid Arctic air on their last night. There were no savory aromas of food bubbling in a pot, or even hot tea in a camp kettle hanging over the flames — just a bleak sense of hopelessness.

Removing the branches that covered the men, the three men must have stood looking at their friends with shock and dismay. The gaunt faces of Fitzgerald and Carter, hollowed by extreme privation, faced the cold merciless sky. Their skin was discoloured and black with frostbite. Carter's eyes had been closed, a further indication that he had died first, and Fitzgerald's eyes stared, seemingly resigned to the loss of his world.

Somers, snapping into action, began to perform his police duties. He did a quick search and found a piece of paper in the pocket of Inspector Fitzgerald's pants, on which the following words were written, using a piece of charred wood. Using the charcoal as a makeshift pencil, Fitzgerald's callused and frostbitten hands wrote his last words:

"All money in despatch [sic] bag and bank, clothes, &c, I leave to my dearly beloved mother, Mrs. John Fitzgerald, Halifax. God bless all. F.J Fitzgerald R.N.W.M.P."[3]

Somers found a watch in Constable Carter's pocket, the one he had given to Constable Taylor to be repaired in Dawson. Even in his weakened and desperate state, Taylor's sense of duty never flagged, and he had remembered to give Corporal Somers' watch to Carter to be returned to its rightful owner. Somers continued his search and picked up a blunt axe, a camp kettle, one cup, and three broken snowshoes that were scattered around the area.

Somers and the men then placed the remains of Fitzgerald and Carter on the one large sled they had. After securing the bodies, Peter Ross was detailed to take them back to Fort McPherson. The inspector and Carter, men who had endured the intense loneliness with grit and endurance in the North, where stamina is tied to sanity, were headed to their final resting place. Ross made good time. Arriving back at Fort McPherson by 7:00 p.m., he took the remains to the Church of England Mission to await final preparations for burial. The mood in the community continued to be solemn.

Once Ross was headed north on the Peel River back to Fort McPherson, Somers and Husky headed south for another sixteen kilometres to find and retrieve the remains of Constables Kinney and Taylor. Somers was looking for the blue handkerchief that marked Kinney and Taylor's last camp.

The bodies of the two young officers lay beneath the freshly cut boughs, just as Dempster had left them. Removal of the branches revealed a sad and disturbing sight. Constable Taylor was unrecognizable. His frozen fingers still grasped the rifle that ended his life, a demonstration of the brutal end to the suffering he had endured. Beside him lay Kinney, both men on one sleeping blanket, with two more covering them. When Somers and Husky lifted the corpses onto the two remaining sleds, Somers found their barometer, some old socks, a duffle coat, and some moccasins. He also found the sack containing the diary of Inspector Fitzgerald, which described the terrible and tragic journey of the winter patrol of 1910.[4]

After securing the remains and making a note of all the items at the camp, Somers and Husky made their way back to Fort McPherson. Since it was too far away for one day's travel, the men would be spending the night somewhere along the Peel River homestretch. It so happened that they spent it at the open camp where Fitzgerald and Carter died. It was fitting. Taylor and Kinney would once more be in the same camp as their leader and guide. Just one more night and the four would be united for burial.

Thoughts of better times and playing card games with each other may have consumed the minds of Somers and Husky that evening of March 24. As the snow fell, the dark world closed in around them and their two silent friends. Perhaps Corporal Somers opened the diary and read the daily log kept by the Inspector. He must have had questions as to why the winter patrol had failed. The more he read and understood, the more he would have known about how the patrol carried out their orders and distinguished themselves with their sheer strength and determination to face the ultimate challenge of nature versus man. Once back in Fort McPherson, the full extent of the privation suffered by the four-member winter patrol would be made clear.

Very early the next morning the two men began the last leg of the journey to Fort McPherson. Upon arrival just before noon, they took the bodies to the Church of England Mission, to be placed alongside those of Inspector Fitzgerald and Carter. There, Dempster and Somers began the difficult task of examining the remains. Somers's report on the almost indescribable suffering experienced by Fitzgerald and his men during their desperate effort to return to their starting place leaves nothing to the imagination:

> The bodies of all four were in a terrible emaciated condition. The lower ribs and hip bones showing very prominently. The stomach of each had fallen inwards. The flesh of all was very much discoloured and of a reddish-black colour, and a thin skin seemed to have been peeling off.

All outer clothing was very badly torn and much scorched by fire, the socks, duffels, mitts and moccasins being in the same condition. There is no doubt in my mind that with the exception of Constable Taylor, they all died from starvation and extreme cold.[5]

The report also stated that Kinney's feet had swollen to twice their normal size and one toe had split, exposing raw flesh. Carter's toes were frozen, and hands had been raggedly bandaged and Fitzgerald's toes were slightly frozen and very swollen.[6] Their conditions were grim.

Somers continued with his report, documenting the items each officer had been either wearing or carrying. He had been disturbed to discover that the compass that was given to the inspector the day he left Fort McPherson was now unaccountably missing. Undoubtedly, this would have been one of the reasons why the patrol had not been able to find the designated route.

Basing his judgment on the distance the winter patrol had covered, Somers surmised in his report that Fitzgerald, Carter, Kinney, and Taylor had probably lived for about seven days after the final entry in the inspector's diary. He also recorded that only ten dog harnesses were found. Had the men cut the remaining harnesses into pieces and tried to eat them?

Yukon Archives, 86-42-47.

Four caskets draped with the Union Jack were lowered into the common grave while Somers, Dempster, Fyfe, Turner, and Blake fired the military salute.

After writing his report, Somers, assisted by Reverend C.E. Whittaker, built four coffins with eighty metres of lumber supplied by the Reverend.[7] It was a sombre task. The noise of saws and hammers filled the air, a grating counterpoint to the sound of the metallic ring of shovels hitting the frozen earth. Three First Nations men dug a large grave that would serve as the resting place for the four men. On Sunday, March 26, a special service was held in the Church of England Mission, with the inhabitants of Fort McPherson in attendance and Reverend Whittaker officiating. Together, theirs was the task of giving a final fitting tribute to the deceased.

On March 28, the funeral took place with military honours. An honour guard of five men fired a salute as the coffins were lowered into the frozen grave. The grave would remain open until each coffin had the officers' name attached. Corporal Somers had been given the task of finding a copper kettle for the coffin markers.

Corporal Dempster, Leader Of The R.N.W.M.P. Relief Patrol After Return To Dawson Having Found Remains Of The Lost Fort Mc Pherson To Dawson Patrol.   Photo By J. Doody Dawson Y.T.

RCMP Heritage Centre Archives, P-124/120.

At 1:20 p.m. on April 17, 1911, the relief patrol arrived back in Dawson City. The Dawson City RNWMP detachment then released news of the tragedy, and, within days, newspapers throughout the world carried the story.

Reverend Whittaker wrote to Bishop Stringer in Dawson, praising Inspector Fitzgerald's leadership, saying:

> He was an able and a splendid man in every way. The last evening before leaving he spent with us, and he promised to call and see you all in Dawson. All the members of the patrol are so changed that we should not know them, just famished, and their skin all peeling off.... We had a military funeral....We have buried them in one wide grave, lying side by side. Such a grave has never been here before, and I trust may never be again. The sad event has cast a gloom over the whole place, and we all mourn their loss.[8]

RCMP Heritage Centre Archives, P-124-122.

At 7:00 p.m. on April 16, Jack Dempster's relief patrol arrived at Twelvemile Roadhouse where they made the call to the Dawson City detachment. A fresh dog team was sent to Twelvemile. Dempster arrived in Dawson by 10:30 a.m. and began writing his report. Fyfe, Turner, and Stewart arrived at 1:20 p.m.

Corporal Dempster would be delivering this letter himself when he returned to Dawson City. Dempster and the men left on March 30 to break the sad news to the RNWMP and to a nation. They would make their return in the fastest time ever made on a winter patrol, doing so while spring was changing the terrain around them. They met open water, gale-force winds, heavy trail conditions, mist, snow, and extreme fluctuating temperatures, ranging from -40°C to 17°C above. Despite falling through ice into frigid running water and being almost blinded by blizzards, they carried on, reaching Dawson City on April 17, 1911.

The Dawson City detachment was rocked by the sad news, as were the citizens and First Nations who knew the officers. Telegraph wires hummed as the fate of the winter patrol of 1910–11 was broadcast. A nation mourned, and many must have reflected on the heroic duty that the "Lost Patrol" had undertaken and the ultimate price they had paid for doing so.

They were unyielding as they carried out their duty to the death. Perhaps the most fitting tribute to the men who devoted their lives to the Royal Northwest Mounted Police was written in 1904 by Robert W. Service:

In the little Crimson Manual it's written plain and clear
That who would wear the scarlet coat shall say good-bye to fear;
Shall be a guardian of the right, a sleuth-hound of the trail —
In the little Crimson Manual there's no such word as "fail" —
Shall follow on though heavens fall, or hell's top-turrets freeze,
Half round the world, if need there be, on bleeding hands and knees.
It's duty, duty, first and last, the Crimson Manual saith;
The Scarlet Rider makes reply: "It's duty — to the death."[9]

Epilogue

The news that Dempster took back to Dawson City was shattering. Within days, newspapers across the nation, throughout the United States, and across Great Britain reported on the tragedy. But one of the first to mention the possibility of a disastrous turn of events was a single paragraph in the *Manitoba Free Press*, dated March 7, 1911:

> Four well-known members of the Royal Northwest Mounted Police who went to Fort McPherson and Herschel Island in the Arctic Ocean a week before Christmas, had not on March 1 reached Dawson City, their destination. The party consisted of Sergeant [Inspector] Fitzgerald, Constables Carter, Turner [Taylor] and Kinney. They lost their way along the lower Peel River and Indians guided them for several days to the entrance of the Wind River country, which is only 14 days from Dawson. A relief expedition has gone out from Dawson.

A month later, the fate of the patrol was still in the newspapers. The *Lethbridge Herald* reported on April 8, 1911, that "fears are felt here for the safety of a routine police patrol that left Herschell [*sic*] Island last December and has not been seen or heard from since…," but confirmation of the ill-fated patrol was announced on the front page of the *Manitoba Free Press*, April 18, 1911, after receiving the devastating news from RNWMP Headquarters in Regina. Commissioner Perry reported that Fitzgerald "was a particularly fine northern [not decipherable] a man of great resource....and was looked upon as one of the best all-round officers in the force. His tragic death has cast a gloom over headquarters."

Headlines in Indiana announced: "A Tragedy of The Canadian Wilderness, Mounted Police Make A Brave But Futile fight For Life,"[1] and in Texas, "Four Perish in Wilds."[2] Another Indiana newspaper reported: "Perish in Arctic Cold, Bodies of Missing Four Canadian Mounted Police Found."[3] The London, England, newspaper printed the sad news that the search party sent to look for Fitzgerald, Carter, Kinney, and Taylor, "found the four dead bodies of their comrades on the trail twenty-five miles from their destination...."[4]

While the news was announced, Dempster was handed his next set of orders. The RNWMP, under Dempster's leadership, were to make the Dawson to Fort McPherson patrol route safe and recognizable for future mail and dispatch patrols. During 1912–13 Dempster established supply caches of food and built shelter cabins, which eliminated the tiresome work of setting up night camps. But, most importantly, Dempster blazed the trail by making "lobsticks." The trees known as "lobsticks" were stripped bare except for their top branches and two branches sticking out lower down, making them evident as trail markers. Lobsticks, however, could easily be blown down in a windstorm, burned in a forest fire, or even be covered in wet snow. First Nations guides were also taken on every subsequent winter patrol and a two-week intensive training program was initiated for any new member before leaving Dawson City on winter patrol.

Jack Dempster, a man who understood and respected the forces of nature, truly owned the title of "Iron Man of the Trail." Before the end of his time served in the Yukon was over he set the fastest time of fourteen days on the patrol route from Dawson City to Fort McPherson.

During the year following the death of the Fitzgerald winter patrol, while Dempster was on the trail making it safe, all aspects of the tragedy were examined by an official inquiry. The conclusion identified three simple causes that led to the disaster:

1. The small quantity of provisions taken,
2. Want of an efficient guide,
3. Delay in searching for the lost trail.[5]

The winter patrols continued between Dawson to Fort McPherson until 1921 with no further loss of life.

On February 13, 1985, seventy-five years after the tragedy known as the "Lost Patrol," a group of eleven Yukoners, two of whom were active serving members of the Royal Canadian Mounted Police, decided to recreate the ill-fated patrol of Inspector Fitzgerald. Their adventure would rival any reality television survival show.

The group left Whitehorse, Yukon, in a rented van to travel the 1,127 kilometres to Fort McPherson. They travelled through the area with mountains now bearing the names of the Lost Patrol, and they drove along the Dempster Highway, named after Jack Dempster, to their starting destination of Fort McPherson.

The undertaking was monumental. Eleven men, forty-seven dogs, four snow mobiles, approximately 3,500 pounds of food, plus all the camping gear, tents, axes, cooking utensils, and any other items they felt they needed. Spirits were high and the enthusiastic group was keen and ready to get on the road after a year of planning. Since Dempster had set the record of fourteen days, this group planned a fifteen-day patrol.

RCMP Sergeant D.G. Pittendreigh led the group. The dogs were safely housed in wooden crates stacked in the van and the expedition headed along the Dempster Highway. Sergeant Pittendreigh wrote in his diary: "Little did we know that within 12 hours of starting out, 'mother nature' and Canada's northern wilderness would show us, in no uncertain terms, just how severely man and machine could be tested."[6]

After a mere three hours on the highway, the rented van broke down. Some members of the patrol sustained minor frostbite while they waited for highway help. It took the group another three hours to arrive at Eagle Plains Lodge (a complex built on a plateau on the Dempster Highway), where they unloaded the dogs and tied them out on their lines. The dogs, like the hard-working patrol dogs from early in the century, were a priority and were given water and fed upon arrival.

The daily struggles of Pittendreigh's patrol provides an insight into the conditions that even with modern day conveniences is no guarantee for success. The sergeant recorded that two of the dog boxes were open and empty when they arrived at Fort McPherson. "Great panic" ensued, and finally someone noticed that four dogs had been "stuffed" into two boxes!

On February 16, 1985, in a -40°C temperature under clear and calm skies they realized their delay in Eagle Plains had cost them two days of food supplies and that they would be starting their trip short of supplies. Another day was spent in Fort McPherson as they gathered more provisions, but spirits were still high. The following day, Sunday, February 17, eleven people and with additional dogs now numbering fifty-four, with four snowmobile engines running and leading the way, pulled out of Fort McPherson.

The group travelled a distance of forty kilometres their first day and twenty-two kilometres on their second. On this day the sergeant wrote: "Cutting and hauling wood is a full-time job for three people."[7] February 19 saw temperatures reach a low of -54°C, which was too cold for travel. They were burning two cord of wood per day to cook and keep warm, and the snowmobiles were using twice the amount of fuel as had been anticipated. The group realized they were not going to make their first cache without more fuel and dog food. They decided to turn back and get more supplies from Fort McPherson.

It would take them two days to retrace their steps and return to their starting point. The sergeant recorded: "February 20th was no better than the day before. The tent is heavily coated in ice, causing dripping on the inside and most bedding is soaked."[8] Things were going from bad to worse, and, upon reaching Fort McPherson, some members of the expedition decided to give up and head back to Whitehorse. Pittendreigh and the remaining others (there is nothing in his log that said how many were left in the expedition) would depart again with replenished supplies and meet their First Nations guide, Simon Snowshoe, his two sons, and their dog teams, 120 kilometres downriver from Fort McPherson. The next part of their patrol would prove as difficult as the first few days.

Finally, on Tuesday, February 26, the smaller group got underway at 9:30 a.m. The temperature had warmed to -23°C and the soft powdery snow was over one metre deep on the river trail. They travelled for two hours, then stopped for lunch, at the base of the 250-metre hill they had to climb. After lunch, the men attached the toboggans to the snowmobiles and attempted the climb. They failed. The snow was too deep for the machines, so they decided to use the dogs to haul the supplies. It took the group an exhausting five-and-a half hours to reach the top.

At this point more members of the expedition decided that they too had had enough and decided to head back to Fort McPherson. This left just one person to carry on with the First Nations guide and the remaining dogs, but only for a further eighty kilometres before he also gave up. The expedition attempted seventy-five years later succumbed to the forces of nature. It was nature that still determined who would be permitted to travel in the Yukon wilds.

Pittendreigh summed up his attempt:

> The trip as planned was not a success. Failure is never easy to accept but I do feel we had some success in bringing the entire thing together .... Despite the cold, we did learn a great deal of appreciation for the North and "mother nature" ... I paused to sit beside Fitzgerald's final resting place and found myself feeling very close to four men I will never meet. Their strength and endurance amazed me.[9]

Constable C. R. Thornback summed up a constable's duty while training for his patrol in 1914. He wrote:

> We learned how to handle our dogs, how to harness and drive them, unharness and care for them, prepare their food and feed them. Before the end of our training period, men and dogs were in top physical condition. We were under constant surveillance for any sign of inability or show of weakness that might endanger the lives of others of the patrol. So much depended on perfection.[10]

FORT McPHERSON, NWT

GRAVE OF THE
LOST PATROL

Yukon Archives, 2009-10-100.

The original headstones have now been changed and the grave is marked with the names of all four men, Fitzgerald, Carter, Kinney, and Taylor, on a large stone cross dominating the St. Mathews Anglican Church cemetery in Fort McPherson, Northwest Territories.

Perfection is the highest degree of excellence, or the highest degree of proficiency. Officers were and are expected to perform to the highest degree of excellence and be proficient in their duty, but they were then and are now human. The men who protected and helped build our nation were men just like any other, and behind their badges were hearts that beat just like the hearts of other people. They lived, laughed, and loved, but unlike anyone else, they had taken an oath to lay down their lives for their sworn duty — extraordinary individuals, standing watch together as they uphold the rights of all who live on Canadian soil. The same is true of peace officers today.

Fitzgerald, Kinney, Carter, and Taylor exemplified the values of the Royal Northwest Mounted Police. They were unyielding as they carried out their duty to the death. They strived for perfection. A small grave in Canada's remote North is the final resting place honoring the four men. It is the perfect place to rest, for these men who died on duty to protect Canada's borders. Historian Dick North quotes Inspector George French of the Royal Northwest Mounted Police who summarized the duties of the members of the force by saying, "I demand that neither hardship, suffering, privation, nor fear of death should move you by a hair's breadth from carrying out your duties."[11] North himself summarized the epic story of the Lost Patrol by saying their tragedy was "where legend and reality become one."[12]

APPENDIX A
Chronology of
Francis Joseph Fitzgerald

F.J. Fitzgerald.

RCMP Heritage Centre Archives.

APRIL 12, 1869: Born in Halifax, Nova Scotia.

1887: Charted an overland route from Edmonton to Fort Selkirk, Yukon, via northern British Columbia, covering 1,600 kilometres.

NOVEMBER 19, 1888: Joined the North West Mounted Police as Constable, Regimental No. 2218.

1899: Promoted to Corporal.

1900–01: Served with the 2nd Canadian Mounted Rifles during the Boer War and was awarded the Queen's South African Medal.

1902: Established the first detachments at Fort McPherson and Herschel Island, Yukon Territories.

AUGUST 9, 1902: Represented the NWMP at the coronation of His Majesty King Edward VII in England and was awarded the King Edward VII Coronation Medal.

1903: Promoted to Sergeant.

1905: Promoted to Staff Sergeant.

APRIL 26, 1906: Received a letter of appreciation from NWMP Commissioner Aylesworth Bowen Perry for dedication to duty on the Dawson to Fort McPherson winter patrol under extreme conditions.

1909–10: Promoted to Inspector.

1910: Selected for the contingent to be sent to London, England for the coronation of King George V, scheduled for June 22, 1911.

APPROXIMATELY FEBRUARY 14, 1911: Died as a member of the Lost Patrol, at age forty-three.

Francis Fitzgerald served twenty-three years with the force (1888–1911), as a member of the NWMP and later the RNWMP, displaying exemplary dedication throughout, in all aspects of the preservation of peace and lawfulness in the Dominion. This reputation earned him his name as the Mounties' "Northern Man." This book is his story as he made his way south from Fort McPherson to Dawson City to join the contingent travelling to the coronation of King George V.

APPENDIX B
Chronology of
W.J.D. "Jack" Dempster

W.J.D. "Jack" Dempster

OCTOBER 21, 1876: Born in Fishguard, South Wales.

1897: Joined the North West Mounted Police, as Constable, Regimental No. 3193.

JANUARY 1911: Promoted to Corporal.

1911: Gained international attention with his leadership of the search party for Fitzgerald's Lost Patrol. Dempster's efforts during the relief patrol earned him the name of the "Iron Man of the Trail."

MAY 1912: Promoted to Sergeant.

JULY 1918: Promoted to Staff Sergeant.

MAY 1931: Promoted to Inspector.

1934: Retired from Royal Canadian Mounted Police.

1959: Construction begins on Dempster Highway, named after Jack Dempster. The 671 kilometre all-weather highway, running from Dawson City, Yukon, to Fort McPherson Northwest Territories, was officially opened in 1979.

OCTOBER 25, 1964: Died in Vancouver, British Columbia, at age eighty-seven.

Jack Dempster served for thirty-seven years in Canada's North, where he gained tremendous respect for his commitment to "maintaining the right" in several Yukon communities. During this time, he formed unique relationships with the northern Aboriginal people and learned from them how to meet the incomparable challenges that the North can and does present.

Notes

INTRODUCTION

1. "The Royal Ulster Constabulary GC," Royal Irish Constabulary (1814–1922), *www.royalirishconstabulary.com/*, accessed March 9, 2012.
2. "Royal Canadian Mounted Police Depot Chapel," Parks Canada Agency Canadian Register of Historic Places, *www.historicplaces.ca/en/rep-reg/place-lieu.aspx?id=15982*, accessed April 23, 2013.
3. Dick North, *The Lost Patrol: The Mounties' Yukon Tragedy* (Vancouver: Raincoast Books, 1995), 4.

CHAPTER 1: TETL'IT ZHEH: THE STORY BEGINS

1. "Fort McPherson: A Brief History," Hamlet of Fort McPherson, *www.fortmcpherson.ca/AboutUs*, accessed September 13, 2012.
2. *Ibid.*
3. Depot Division Library, Regina, Saskatchewan, RCMP, Sessional Papers, 1911. Paper No. 28, March 17, 1910, and Sessional Paper No. 28, Appendix D, I George V, A. 1911.
4. *Ibid.*
5. Elle Andra-Warner, *The Mounties: Tales of Adventure and Danger from the Early Days* (Vancouver: Heritage House Publishing Company, 2009), 104.

6. Chris Conger, "Why Wolves Howl," Animal Planet, *http://animal.discovery. com/mammals/wolves-howling-at-moon1.htm*, accessed September 13, 2013.

CHAPTER 2: EVENINGS OF STORYTELLING

1. Quote taken from an interactive display featured at the Royal Canadian Mounted Police Heritage Centre, Regina, Saskatchewan.
2. "Why the North West Mounted Police Was Formed," Our Heritage, *www.ourheritage.net/index_page_stuff/Following_Trails/NWMP_ Background/whynwmpformed.html*, last updated July 17, 2012.
3. Philip Goldring, "Cypress Hills Massacre," the Canadian Encyclopedia, *www.thecanadianencyclopedia.com/featured/cypress-hills-massacre*, accessed November 8, 2012.
4. Tony Hollihan, *The Mounties March West: The Epic Trek and Early Adventures of the Mounted Police* (Edmonton: Folklore Publishing, 2004), 9.
5. *Ibid.*, 9.
6. *Ibid.*, 16.
7. "The Royal Ulster Constabulary GC," Royal Irish Constabulary (1814– 1922), *www.royalirishconstabulary.com/*, accessed March 9, 2012.
8. Hollihan, *The Mounties March West*, 12.
9. *Ibid.*, 15.
10. "The Origins of the Royal Canadian Mounted Police," published by the Royal Canadian Mounted Police National Services Directorate, Ottawa, 2002, *www.rcmp-grc.gc.ca/pdfs/origins-debuts-eng.pdf*, accessed January 5, 2013.
11. Rodger D. Touchie, *Bear Child: The Life and Times of Jerry Potts* (Vancouver: Heritage House Publishing Company, 2005), 143.
12. Hollihan, *The Mounties March West*, 97.
13. Bill Bryson, *At Home: A Short History of Private Life* (Toronto: Anchor Canada, 2011) 298.
14. Touchie, *Bear Child*, 143.
15. *Ibid.*, 143.
16. "Potts, Jerry," Dictionary of Canadian Biography Online, *www.biographi. ca/009004-119.01-e.php?id_nbr=6372*, accessed November 8, 2012.

17. The Mounties or the RCMP, *www.k12studycanada.org/files/History%20 of%20the%20RCMP.pdf,* last updated March 2003.
18. Library and Archives Canada, "Without Fear, Favour, or Affection: The Men of the North West Mounted Police," *www.lac-bac.gc.ca/ nwmp-pcno/025003-1302-e.html,* last modified October 31, 2012.
19. *Ibid.*
20. *Ibid.*
21. *Ibid.*

CHAPTER 3: LOST AND FOUND

1. Robert W. Service, "The Land God Forgot," accessed August 30, 2013, *www.poemhunter.com/poem/the-land-god-forgot/.*
2. Jerry Vanek DVM, "Yukon Quest Sled Dogs: The Mathematics of Mushing," Yukon Quest, *www.yukonquest.com/site/mathematics-of-mushing,* accessed January 20, 2013.
3. Fitzgerald made the daily entry in his logbook. Since leaving Fort McPherson, they had travelled 105 kilometres.
4. Edward Butts, *Line of Fire: Heroism, Tragedy, and Canada's Police* (Toronto: Dundurn, 2009), 90.
5. Carlos Barceló, Stefano Liberati, Sebastiano Sonego, and Matt Visser, "How Quantum Effects could Create Black Stars, Not Holes," *www. scientificamerican.com/article.cfm?id=black-stars-not-holes,* accessed April 22, 2013.

CHAPTER 4: ESAU GEORGE GUIDES THE PATROL

1. Robert W. Service, "The Law Of The Yukon," accessed August 30, 2013, *www.poemhunter.com/poem/the-law-of-the-yukon/.*
2. Depot Division Library, Regina, Saskatchewan, RCMP Sessional Papers No. 28, 1910 and 1911.
3. "Sir John A. Macdonald and the North West Mounted Police," Royal Canadian Mounted Police, *www.rcmp-grc.gc.ca/hist/ori-deb/debuts1-eng. htm,* last updated September 1, 2002.

4. "The Origins of the Royal Canadian Mounted Police," published by Royal Canadian Mounted Police Public National Communication Services Directorate, 2002, *www.rcmp-grc.gc.ca/pdfs/origins-debuts-eng.pdf*, accessed January 5, 2013.

5. "Glacial Refugia," Northwest Territories Protected Strategy, *www.nwtpas.ca/science-glacialrefugia.asp*, last updated July 2012, and "A View into the Ancient Past," Yukon Info, *www.yukoninfo.com/whitehorse/milescanyon/past.htm*, accessed April 22, 2013.

6. "Musk-Ox," National Geographic, *http://animals.nationalgeographic.com/animals/mammals/musk-ox/*, accessed April 22, 2013.

7. "The Muskox Patrol: High Arctic Sovereignty Revisited," Info North, *http://pubs.aina.ucalgary.ca/arctic/arctic56-1-101.pdf*, accessed May 7, 2013.

8. "Glacial Refugia," Northwest Territories Protected Strategy, *www.nwtpas.ca/science-glacialrefugia.asp*, last updated July 2012, and "A View into the Ancient Past," Yukon Info, *www.yukoninfo.com/whitehorse/milescanyon/past.htm*, accessed April 22, 2013.

9. "Wolf Spirit Meaning, Symbols and Totem," All Totems, *http://alltotems.com/wolf-totem-symbolism-and-meaning/*, accessed January 20, 2013.

CHAPTER 5: A NEW YEAR

1. Robert W. Service, "The Law Of The Yukon," accessed August 30, 2013, *www.poemhunter.com/poem/the-law-of-the-yukon/*.

2. Butts, *Line Of Fire*, 91.

3. "Klondike Gold Rush," Royal Canadian Mounted Police, *www.rcmp-grc.gc.ca/hist/ori-deb/debuts10-eng.htm*, accessed December 3, 2012.

4. "The Origins of the Royal Canadian Mounted Police," published by Royal Canadian Mounted Police Public National Communication Services Directorate, 2002.

5. *Ibid.*

CHAPTER 6: THE PEEL RIVER CANYON

1. Robert W. Service, "The Law Of The Yukon," accessed August 30, 2013, *www.poemhunter.com/poem/the-law-of-the-yukon/*.

2. Andra-Warner, *The Mounties*, 104.
3. *Ibid.*
4. *Ibid.*

CHAPTER 7: THE WRATH OF NATURE

1. Robert W. Service, "The Spell of the Yukon," accessed August 20, 2013, see *freemasonry.bcy.ca/biography/service_r_w/spell_yukon.html*.
2. "Know Your Mushing Terms," Athropolis Facts: Cold, Icy, and Arctic, *www.athropolis.com/arctic-facts/fact-dogs-command.htm*, accessed May 7, 2013.
3. Andra-Warner, *The Mounties*, 101.
4. *Ibid.*, 89.

CHAPTER 8: ARCTIC DEEP FREEZE

1. Robert W. Service, "Men of the High North," accessed August 20, 2013, see *www.internal.org/Robert_W_Service/Men_of_the_High_North.com*.
2. "The Wind River," Canoeing the Wind River with Sila Sojourns, *www.silasojourns.com/trips/wind.html*, accessed May 5, 2013.
3. "Legends and Folklore of the Northern Lights," Indigenous Peoples' Literature, *www.indigenouspeople.net/aurora.htm*, last modified July 29, 2007.

CHAPTER 9: FORREST CREEK TURNOFF

1. Robert W. Service, "The Lone Trail," accessed August 30, 2013, *www.poemhunter.com/poem/the-lone-trail/*.
2. Beth Dempster, email to author, June 5, 2013.

CHAPTER 10: "MY LAST HOPE IS GONE"

1. Dick North, *The Lost Patrol: The Mounties' Yukon Tragedy* (Vancouver: Raincoast Books, 1995), 96.

2. Anniina Jokinen, "Aurora Borealis: The Northern Lights, in Mythology and Folklore," Luminarium, *www.luminarium.org/mythology/revontulet.htm*, accessed February 14, 2013.

CHAPTER 11: THE STRUGGLE CONTINUES
1. Robert W. Service, "The Spell of the Yukon," accessed August 20, 2013, see *freemasonry.bcy.ca/biography/service_r_w/spell_yukon.html*.
2. "Inuit Mythology," Wikipedia contributors, Wikipedia, *en.wikipedia.org/wiki/Inuit* mythology, last modified February 26, 2013.

CHAPTER 12: LOSING THE RACE
1. Robert W. Service, "Carry On! Carry On!," accessed August 20, 2103, see *http://freemasonry.bcy.ca/biography/service_r_w/carry_on.html*.

CHAPTER 13: DUTY TO THE DEATH
1. Robert W. Service, "Clancy of the Mounted Police," accessed August 20, 2013, see *www.robertwservice.com/modules/smartsection/item.php?itemid=79&keywords=clancy+the+mounted+police*.
2. Depot Division Library, Regina, Saskatchewan, RCMP, Sessional Papers, 1911.
3. *Ibid.*
4. *Ibid.*
5. *Ibid.*

CHAPTER 14: IRON MAN OF THE TRAIL
1. "The Lost Patrol 1911: Fifty Years Later, 1961," *The Scarlet and Gold Magazine* (1961), *http://freepages.genealogy.rootsweb.ancestry.com/~edmund howard/HowardEL/THE%20LOST%20PATROL.htm*, accessed March 9, 2013.
2. Depot Division Library, Regina, Saskatchewan, RCMP, Sessional Papers, 1911.

3. *Ibid.*

4. Ken Spotswood, "Dempster Decision," Yukon Info.com, *www.yukoninfo. com/dempster/thename.htm*, accessed January 20, 2013.

5. Depot Division Library, Regina, Saskatchewan, RCMP Sessional Papers, 1911.

6. Butts, *Line Of Fire*, 87.

7. Depot Division Library, Regina, Saskatchewan, RCMP Sessional Papers, 1911.

8. Ogden Tanner, *The Old West: The Canadians* (Alexandria, Virginia: Time-Life Books, 1977), 177.

CHAPTER 15: ASCENDING THE GLACIERS

1. Robert W. Service, "To the Man of the High North," accessed August 20, 2013, see *www.poemhunter.com/poem/to-the-man-of-the-high-north/*.

2. Beth Dempster, email message to the author, March 13, 2013.

3. Andra-Warner, *The Mounties*, 104.

CHAPTER 16: THE FIRST CLUE

1. "Policing the plains; being the real-life record of the famous Royal North-West Mounted Police," *archive.org/stream/policingplainsbe00mac buoft/policingplainsbe00macbuoft_djvu.txt*, accessed June 13, 2013.

2. "Seal Boy," Avataq Cultural Institute Northern Delights, *www.delice boreal.com/en/nunavik/legends/06.php*, accessed March 9, 2013.

3. "Why the Stars are in the Sky," First People: The Legends, *www.first people.us/FP-Html-Legends/WhyTheStarsAreInTheSky-Eskimo.html*, accessed March 28, 2013.

CHAPTER 17: FOLLOWING THE TRAIL

1. Robert W. Service, "A Song of Winter Weather," accessed August 21, 2013, see *www.poemhunter.com/poem/a-song-of-winter-weather*.

2. Sheila Dempster Calvert, email message to the author, March 22, 2013.

CHAPTER 18: THE LOST PATROL

1. Robert W. Service, "The Trail Of No Return," accessed August 30, 2013, *www.poemhunter.com/poem/the-trail-of-no-return/*.

CHAPTER 19: THE LITTLE CRIMSON MANUAL

1. "Policing the plains being the real-life record of the famous Royal North-West Mounted Police," *archive.org/stream/policingplainsbe00macbuoft/policingplainsbe00macbuoft_djvu.txt*, accessed June 13, 2013.
2. North, *The Lost Patrol*, 108.
3. Depot Division Library, Regina, Saskatchewan, RCMP, Sessional Papers, 1911.
4. North, *The Lost Patrol*, 111.
5. *Ibid.*
6. Depot Division Library, Regina, Saskatchewan, RCMP. Sessional Papers, 1911.
7. *Ibid.*
8. "THE LOST PATROL, 1911-Fifty Years Later-1961, extracted from *The Scarlet & Gold Magazine*, 1961," Learning Centers at *ancestry.com*, accessed March 10, 2013, see *http://freepages.genealogy.rootsweb.ancestry.com/~edmundhoward/HowardEL/THE%20LOST %20PATROL.htm*.
9. "Clancy of the Mounted Police," *RobertWService.com*, accessed March 30, 2013, see *www.robertwservice.com/modules/smartsection/item.php?itemid=79&keywords=clancy+the+mounted+police*.

EPILOGUE

1. "A Tragedy of the Canadian Wilderness," *Fort Wayne News*, April 18, 1911, 16.
2. "Four Perish in Wilds," *Texan San Antonio Light and Gazette*, April 18, 1911, 6.
3. "Perish in Arctic Cold, Bodies of Missing Four Canadian Mounted Police Found," *Indiana Evening Gazette*, April 19, 1911, 4.
4. "Frozen to Death, Fate of Four Mounted Police," *Hackney Express and Shoreditch Observer*, April 22, 1911, 2.

5. Depot Division Library, Regina, Saskatchewan, RCMP Sessional Papers, 1911.

6. "The Commemorative Trip of the 'Lost Patrol' of 1910–1911," *RCMP Quarterly*, Winter (1986): 33–37.

7. *Ibid.*

8. *Ibid.*

9. *Ibid.*

10. North, *The Lost Patrol*, 133.

11. *Ibid.*, xiii.

12. *Ibid.*, 4.

Bibliography

ARTICLES

Schledermann, Peter. "The Muskox Patrol: High Arctic Sovereignty Revisited." *Arctic*, vol. 56, no.1. The Arctic Science and Technology Information System (ASTIS). March 2003: 101–09. *http://pubs.aina. ucalgary.ca/arctic/arctic56-1-101.pdf.*

BOOKS

Anderson, Ian. *Sitting Bull's Boss: Above the Medicine Line with James Morrow Walsh*. Vancouver: Heritage House, 2000.

Andra-Warner, Elle. *The Mounties: Tales of Adventure and Danger from the Early Days*. Vancouver: Heritage House Publishing Company, 2009.

Batchelor, Bruce T. *Nine Dog Winter*. Victoria: Agio Publishing House, 1981.

Butts, Edward. *Line Of Fire: Heroism, Tragedy, and Canada's Police*. Toronto: Dundurn, 2009.

Hollihan, Tony. *The Mounties March West: The Epic Trek and Early Adventures of the Mounted Police*. Edmonton: Folklore Publishing, 2004.

North, Dick. *The Lost Patrol, the Mounties' Yukon Tragedy*. Vancouver: Raincoast Books, 1995.

Tanner, Ogden. *The Old West: The Canadians*. Alexandria, Virginia: Time-Life Books, 1977.

Touchie, Rodger D. *Bear Child: The Life and Times of Jerry Potts*. Vancouver: Heritage House Publishing Company, 2005.

EMAILS

Calvert, Sheila. Email message to the author. March 22, 2013.
Dempster, Beth. Email message to the author. March 13, 2013.

REPORTS

Minister, Public Works and Government Services Canada. *The Origins of the Royal Canadian Mounted Police*. Ottawa: Royal Canadian Mounted Police Public National Communication Services Directorate, 2002.

SESSIONAL PAPERS

Canada. RCMP. Sessional Papers, 1911. Paper No. 28, Constable W.J.D. Dempster, March 17, 1910. Sessional Paper No. 28, Appendix D, I George V, A. 1911.
Canada. Royal Northwest Mounted Police. Sessional Papers, Regina, May 19, 1910. Sessional Paper No. 126, Reports of McPherson-Dawson Patrol, Winter 1910–11.

WEBSITES

Adventure Learning Foundation. "Klondike Gold Rush, Yukon Territory 1897." Accessed December 3, 2012. *www.questconnect.org/ak_klondike. htm.*
All Totems. "Wolf Spirit Meaning, Symbols and Totem." Accessed January 20, 2013. *http://alltotems.com/wolf-totem-symbolism-and-meaning/.*
"Anirniit." Ghostly Tales of Terror. Accessed March 14, 2013. *http://ghostly talesofterror.wordpress.com/2011/02/04/anirniit/.*
Avataq Cultural Institute Northern Delights. "Seal Boy." Accessed March 9, 2013. *www.deliceboreal.com/en/nunavik/legends/06.php.*
Barceló, Carlos, Stefano Liberati, Sebastiano Sonego, and Matt Visser.

"How Quantum Effects could Create Black Stars, Not Holes." Accessed April 22, 2013. *www.scientificamerican.com/article.cfm?id=black-stars-not-holes.*

Canadian River Expeditions & Nahanni River Adventures. "Wind River." Accessed January 15, 2013. *http://nahanni.com/river/wind-river/.*

Conger, Chris. "Why Wolves Howl." Animal Planet. Accessed September 13, 2013. *http://animal.discovery.com/mammals/wolves-howling-at-moon1.htm.*

Department of Environment and Natural Resources, Government of the Northwest Territories. "Muskox in the NWT." Last updated November 7, 2012. *www.enr.gov.nt.ca/_live/pages/wpPages/Muskox.aspx.*

Dempster Highway, "Dempster Decision." Accessed October 31, 2012. *www.yukoninfo.com/dempster/.*

Dogsled. "Dogsledding 101." Accessed December 15, 2013. *www.dogsled.com/category/dog-sledding/.*

Dictionary of Canadian Biography Online. "Potts, Jerry." Accessed November 8, 2012. *www.biographi.ca/009004-119.01-e.php?id_nbr=6372.*

First People: The Legends. "Why the Stars are in the Sky." Accessed March 28, 2013. *www.firstpeople.us/FP-Html-Legends/WhyTheStarsAreInTheSky-Eskimo.html.*

Goldring, Philip. "Cypress Hills Massacre." The Canadian Encyclopedia. Accessed November 8, 2012. *www.thecanadianencyclopedia.com/featured/cypress-hills-massacre.*

Hamlet of Fort McPherson. "Fort McPherson — A Brief History." Accessed September 13, 2012. *www.fortmcpherson.ca/AboutUs.*

Indigenous Peoples' Literature. "Legends and Folklore of the Northern Lights." Last modified July 29, 2007. *www.indigenouspeople.net/aurora.htm.*

Jokinen, Anniina. "Aurora Borealis: The Northern Lights, in Mythology and Folklore." Luminarium. Accessed February 14, 2013. *www.luminarium.org/mythology/revontulet.htm.*

Learning Centers at *ancestry.com.* "THE LOST PATROL, 1911 — Fifty Years Later 1961, Extracted from The Scarlet & Gold Magazine 1961." Accessed March 10, 2013. *http://freepages.genealogy.rootsweb.ancestry.com/~edmundhoward/HowardEL/THE%20LOST%20PATROL.htm.*

Library and Archives Canada. "Without Fear, Favour, or Affection — The Men of the North West Mounted Police." Last Modified October 31, 2012. *www.lac-bac.gc.ca/nwmp-pcno/025003-1302-e.html.*

National Geographic. "Musk-Ox." Accessed April 22, 2013. *http://animals. nationalgeographic.com/animals/mammals/musk-ox/.*

Northwest Territories Protected Strategy. "Glacial Refugia," Last modified July 2012. *www.nwtpas.ca/science-glacialrefugia.asp.*

Our Heritage. "Why the North West Mounted Police Was Formed." Last modified July 17, 2012. *www.ourheritage.net/index_page_stuff/ Following_Trails/NWMP_Background/whynwmpformed.html.*

Parks Canada Agency Canadian Register of Historic Places. "Royal Canadian Mounted Police Depot Chapel." Accessed April 23, 2013. *www.historicplaces.ca/en/rep-reg/place-lieu.aspx?id=15982.*

"Policing the plains being the real-life record of the famous Royal North-West Mounted Police." Accessed June 13, 2013. *archive.org/stream/ policingplainsbe00macbuoft/policingplainsbe00macbuoft_djvu.txt*

RobertWService.com. "Clancy of the Mounted Police." Accessed March 30, 2013. *www.robertwservice.com/modules/smartsection/item.php?itemid =79&keywords=clancy+the+mounted+police.*

Royal Canadian Mounted Police. "Klondike Gold Rush." Accessed December 3, 2012. *www.rcmp-grc.gc.ca/hist/ori-deb/debuts10-eng.htm.*

Royal Canadian Mounted Police. "Sir John A. Macdonald and the North West Mounted Police." Last updated September 1, 2002. *www.rcmp-grc. gc.ca/hist/ori-deb/debuts1-eng.htm.*

Royal Irish Constabulary (1814–1922). "The Royal Ulster Constabulary GC." Accessed March 9, 2013. *www.royalirishconstabulary.com/index3.html.*

Sights and Sites of the Yukon. "Rivers." Accessed January 4, 2013. *www. sightsandsites.ca/northern/dempster/dempster.html.*

Spotswood, Ken. "Dempster Decision." Yukon Info.com. Accessed January 19, 2013. *www.yukoninfo.com/dempster/thename.htm.*

Vanek, Jerry DVM. "Yukon Quest Sled Dogs, The Mathematics of Mushing." Yukon Quest. Accessed January 20, 2013. *www.yukonquest.com/site/ mathematics-of-mushing.*

Wikipedia. "Inuit Mythology." Last modified February 26, 2013. *en.wikipedia. org/wiki/Inuit mythology.*

Bibliography

Yin, Sophia DVM, MS. "Cold Weather Safety for Dogs: Insights from a Sled Dog Veterinarian." Last modified January 18, 2011. *http://drsophiayin.com/blog/entry/cold-weather-safety-for-dogsinsights-from-a-sled-dog-veterinarian.*

Yukon Info. "A View into the Ancient Past." Accessed April 22, 2013. *www.yukoninfo.com/whitehorse/milescanyon/past.htm.*

Index

Numbers in italics refer to images and their captions.

About the Author

Photo by Shannon Rickman

Kerry Karram grew up in British Columbia at the foot of Grouse Mountain. Hiking mountain trails and observing wildlife instilled in her a love for nature. As she walked with her grandmother, Kerry listened to stories about her life in the Yukon, and later came upon letters written by her grandfather, Constable Andrew D. Cruickshank (Re. # 9959), describing his life as a Royal Canadian Mounted Police officer in the early 1920s. Stories of his extraordinary experiences, especially those in the Canadian Arctic, ignited her interest in the accounts of those brave men and women who contributed so much to the early history of Canada, particularly to the Canadian North. This interest prompted her to write her first book, *Four Degrees Celsius: A Story of Arctic Peril.*

In *Death Wins in the Arctic: The Lost Winter Patrol of 1910*, Kerry uses the handwritten diary of Royal Northwest Mounted Police Inspector F.J. Fitzgerald to chronicle the harrowing ordeal of four RNWMP officers lost in the Yukon wilderness for fifty-two days during the winter of 1910–11. The epic story of the winter patrol is combined with the journal kept by Corporal Jack Dempster, the Mountie in charge of the search for the four missing officers. These books demonstrate her deep interest in Canadian history and her love for the North. Kerry lives in North Vancouver with her husband Michael and their children.